Test-Savvy Math
Fostering Thinking and Reasoning into the Test-Prep Process

By Christine King

www.ckingeducation.com

Produced for C. King Education, Inc. by Christine Mulgrave-King

Copyright © 2013 C. King Education, Inc., Christine Mulgrave-King.

Permission to Reproduce
All rights reserved. No part of the book may be reproduced in any form, stored in a retrieval system, by any mechanical, photocopying, recording, scanning, electronic means, or otherwise under Section 107 or 108 of the 1976 United States Copyright Act, without prior written permission of C. King Education, Inc.

Permission is given to individual classroom teachers to reproduce the pages for classroom instruction use only. Reproduction of these materials for an entire school or district is strictly forbidden.

All web links in this book are correct as the publication date below, but may become inactive or otherwise modified since that time. If you notice a deactivated or changed link, please email books@ckingeducation.com with the words "Links Update – Test-Savvy Math" in the subject line. In your message, please specify the web link and page number on which the link appears.

For additional copies of this publication or permission to reproduce this work, please contact:

C. King Education, Inc.
Tel. 412-CKingEd
Email: publications@ckingeducation.com
Website: www.ckingeducation.com

Test-Savvy, Test-Savvy Math are trademarks of C. King Education, Inc. All rights reserved.

Printed in the United States of America through CreateSpace, LLC

Cover Design by Christine Mulgrave-King

ISBN-13: 978-1468137576
ISBN-10: 1468137573
Publication Date: June 2013

*For all the educators who believe that test-preparation
and sound instruction can go hand-in-hand.*

*For all the students who can't wait until the
day after testing, so that school can be fun again.*

*For all the parents who just want their children to
get a good education that will prepare them to think critically.*

Acknowledgements

This book would not have been possible without the support, encouragement, and feedback from my colleagues and friends Dr. Nicki Newton and Dr. Janine Stewart, both of whom constantly reminded me that I needed to share these ideas with teachers.

I would also like to thank the following people for helping to make this book possible:

My husband, Angelo King, for having a great last name and for taking care of me, so that I could take care of others. My mother and business manager, Beverly Finney, for being courageous enough to take this journey with me and for having faith in me and my abilities. Thanks, Mum. My niece, Sequoia Mulgrave, for being that shining light who looks at me like, "Aunty, you can do anything."

Thanks, Chris Copeland for always pushing me, even when I push back. Thanks, John Sasko for always believing in me and being willing to read and re-read time and time again. Thanks, Ashley Kilburn for taking the time to thoroughly read and edit this book while taking care of your little one. Thanks, Sharon Leboa for always being a source of positive, constructive feedback.

I would like to thank all the teachers that I have worked with over the years, particularly those who have inspired me to develop additional strategies. I thank the ones who were always willing to have-a-go at a new strategy and suggest ways to improve. Also, the teachers whose excitement at workshops inspired me to complete this book. I would especially like to acknowledge Vyviane Le, whose feedback and enthusiasm has been invaluable in bringing forth this book.

Finally, I am indebted to Cecilia Jackson, Meredith Gotlin, Roshone Ault-Le, Andrea Lawrence, and Velma Gunn for providing the opportunity for me to share the ideas contained in this book with their teachers and for making it a priority expectation that we teach our students how to think.

About This Book

Test-Savvy Math: Fostering Thinking and Reasoning into the Test-Prep Process is designed to help teachers by providing practical, year-long, interactive activities to develop students' test-taking skills, while helping to build critical thinking skills. It includes 25 research-based strategies that embody and bring to life the Common Core State Standard (CCSS) Mathematical Practices. Each strategy incorporates some or all elements of student collaboration, student-ownership, accountable talk, error analysis, and tapping into ones prior knowledge. The strategies detailed within this book are outlined using a step-by-step process. Learning objectives, guiding questions, extension ideas, and assessment opportunities are also included. *Test-Savvy Math: Fostering Thinking and Reasoning into the Test-Prep Process* is meant to work in conjunction with your existing curriculum materials and test-prep resources.

Contents

Acknowledgements	v
About This Book	vii
Introduction	1
What Teachers are Saying	2
How to Use this Book	3
Activity Overview	4
Fostering Test-Savvy Students	5
• Test-Savvy Principles	5
• How Students Learn to Become Better Test-Takers	7
• General Trends Of Standardized Exams and Implications for Instruction	8
• Testing in the Age of the Common Core State Standards	9
• Evidence-Centered Design Impact On Instruction	11
• How Test-Savvy Math Addresses the Rigors of an Evidence-Centered Design Model for the CCSSM	13
Getting Started	14
• Becoming a Test-Savvy Teacher	14
• The First Steps	14
• Finding Problems to Use	15
• Implementing a Test-Savvy Strategy	15
• Gathering Data and Documenting Progress	15
• Actively Incorporating the Mathematical Practices	16
• Ideas for Lead Teachers, Coaches and Administrators	16
• Ideas for Curriculum Coordinators and Districts	16
Quick Glance	18
Common Core State Standards Mathematical Practices	20
NCTM Process Standards	22
Section 1: Year-long Test-Savvy Activities	23
Building Critical Thinking Skills	
1. Word Problem Rework	24
2. Rate My Work	29
3. Find and Fix My Error	31

4.	Word Problem Carousel	33
5.	Question Category	35
6.	I Review	39
7.	Two Arguments	41
8.	Collaborative Explanation	43

Section 2: Tapping into Prior Knowledge   45
Knowing What You Know

9.	Concept Square	47
10.	Frayer Model Problem Solving	49
11.	Rally Round the Problem	51

Section 3: Representing Math   53
Showing What You Know

12.	Match the Math Picture	55
13.	Show Me in Many Ways	57
14.	Verbal & Visual Word Association	59
15.	Representing the Operation	61

Section 4: Thinking like a Test-Maker   63
Building Reasoning, Confidence & Stamina

16.	Evaluating the Choices	65
17.	Match the Choices	67
18.	What is the Question?	69
19.	What are the Choices?	71
20.	Multiple-Choice in Minutes	73

Section 5: Vocabulary Games   75
Knowing & Applying Math Terms

21.	Sunflower Word Riddle	77
22.	Vocabulary Tic Tac Toe	79
23.	Word Clusters	81
24.	School Yard Hand Game	83
25.	Mystery Vocabulary	85

Activity Templates   87
Appendix   121
References   134
About the Author   135

Introduction

The goal of this book is to provide educators with practical tools that they can use to help students become more mathematically proficient and concurrently test-savvy by building and strengthening thinking and reasoning skills. *Test-Savvy Math: Fostering Thinking and Reasoning into the Test-Prep Process* is arranged in five sections:

1. Year-long Activities
2. Tapping into Prior Knowledge
3. Representing Math
4. Thinking like a Test-Maker
5. Vocabulary Games

All test-savvy activities share some common characteristics.
- **Foster accountable talk** and opportunities for students to share, naturally and almost automatically.
- **Utilize non-linguistic representations** such as mathematical sketches, diagrams, and mental models.
- **Allow students to tap into their prior knowledge** and generate new ideas, creating stronger mathematical connections and understandings.
- **Require student justification of solutions via collaboration**, while allowing for error analysis and building of in mechanisms to learn from their own mistakes.
- **Embody higher-order thinking skills** via the application of knowledge and/or procedures, analysis of the task presented, **evaluation of the work produced**, and creation using synthesized information to **promote student ownership**.

The activities detailed in this book can be and should be used throughout the school year to build students ability to connect and apply mathematical concepts and skills across domains areas, while analyzing common error patterns made by other students and themselves. All the activities can be adapted for whole class, small-groups or used for independent practice. These activities are rich enough to address and be tailored to all math content areas. Activity Templates are provided for activities and editable versions can be downloaded at ckingeducation.com.

What Teachers Are Saying

"I have to admit that I was expecting something totally different when I heard the words 'test-savvy'. My first impression was that we'd focus on test sophistication skills and strategies such as bubbling, process of elimination, navigating the test, etc. So you can imagine how impressed and eager I was when I learned that you would equip us with tools and strategies to develop kids' conceptual understanding and deepen their overall thinking.

All of the principles and strategies we learned are so valuable in delivering meaningful and engaging instruction. I really enjoyed the hands-on nature of the PD. There are many parallels between this professional development session and my SIOP training. This is profound because when used together, these strategies will enhance my effectiveness in teaching ELLs. The PD offered a great deal of strategies so I will choose a few of the strategies I think my students would benefit from most to implement throughout the rest of the year. We've already launched "Word Problem Rework" in the class and it has been so eye opening to see what my students are capable of and where their misconceptions lie. Thanks so much Christine!" – Rina Mamdouh, K – 5 Teacher

"I've been using the Test-Savvy Strategies for the last four years and it's proven to be the most effective way to prepare middle school students for state exams. Students were able to use the strategies independently after I introduced it to them at the beginning of the year. It's test-prep without pressure and anxiety of test-prep." – Vyviane Le, Middle School Math Teacher

"I am super excited about this book. This is just what we needed. Everyone is hyper-concerned about the upcoming Common Core assessment and how to prepare students for it. This book is part of the answer. Test-Savvy Math gives a long term strategic solution to an ever present dilemma." – Dr. Nicki Newton, Math Consultant, author of "Guided Math in Action: Building Each Student's Mathematical Proficiency with Small-Group Instruction"

"If we taught like this all the time, we would not have to do test-prep." – Ms. Brown, Special Education Teacher

How to Use this Book

BUILDING CRITICAL THINKING SKILLS

"The principle goal of education in the schools should be creating men and women who are capable of doing new things, not simply repeating what other generations have done; men and women who are creative, inventive and discoverers, who can be critical and verify, and not accept, everything they are offered."

- Jean Piaget, Swiss Philosopher and Scientist
"Education for Democracy," Education for Democracy: Proceedings from the Cambridge School Conference on Progressive Education, 1988

Preparation for standardized examinations seems to be in complete conflict with the aforementioned statement. We teach students how to follow rules and apply one procedure to get the answer. But does that have to be the case? Can test preparation prepare students to be citizens who help to solve societal problems? A test-savvy approach argues that the answer to questions on standardized exams, while important, is not the only critical part of taking a test. *Test-Savvy Math: Fostering Thinking and Reasoning into the Test-Prep Process* contends that our processes for thinking about a problem, our flexibility when looking at information presented in new ways and making the accompanying adjustments as needed are the true measure of how much we know and understand.

OVERVIEW OF FORMAT

Test-savvy strategies are outlined as stand-alone activities. For ease of use, all the lessons have a similar format. The lessons include a learning objective, guiding questions that can be asked during the lesson, a summary of the task, materials needed, test-savvy skills addressed by the activity, and an indication of the CCSS Mathematical Practices that are embodied by the strategy. Also included is the set-up, the activity in action, ways to assess the effectiveness of the task, extension ideas, and frequently asked questions (FAQ). Each strategy is followed by a student work sample and/or support materials.

Additionally, you will see opportunities to reflect on current research around how students learn. Excerpts from the Test-Savvy Math Blog can be used as discussion starters. The "Have-a-Go" icon provides an opportunity to try out an activity.

 RESEARCH

 BLOG ENTRY

 HAVE A GO!

Activity Overview

A **Learning Objective** is listed for each activity. This focuses on what we want students to be able to do. Following each learning objective are **Guiding Questions**, which teachers can use to facilitate and deepen student thinking while they are engaged in the activity.

Materials provide a short list of items needed to successfully implement this activity. Most of the activities are followed by a student sample and template. Templates can be found in the back of the book.

Test-Savvy Skills list higher order thinking skills as related to test preparation that the activity provides experiences with and aims to achieve.

Listed are the **Common Core State Standard Mathematical Practices** (see pages 20 – 21) that can be addressed by specific activities.

Each activity lists ideas for **Assessments, Extensions, and FAQ**.

Activity in Action provides clear, concise steps for implementation. Some activities have a **Set Up** prior to the Activity in Action to better help teachers prepare.

Suggested **time** frames are provided to help teachers gauge how to structure their math period. The timings are based upon work done in actual classrooms.

LEARNING OBJECTIVE
Students will be able to solve problems similar to the "Original Problem."

GUIDING QUESTIONS
- Do your numbers make sense given the context/situation? Why?
- How does the problem change?
- How do your changes affect the solution?

MATERIALS
- Template: Word Problem Rework
- a multiple-choice question

TEST-SAVVY SKILLS
- Manipulate mathematical ideas as applied to real-world contexts
- Generate their own problems & solutions
- Discuss/critique solutions
- Identify common misconceptions related to concepts
- Develops visual memory of the exam format
- Is self-reflective, critical of work
- Seeks out, identifies, explains and, replicates errors as tools for learning
- Perseveres, is flexible even when questions are challenging, has alternative strategies

MATHEMATICAL PRACTICES
1. Make sense of problems and persevere in solving them
2. Reason abstractly and quantitatively
3. Construct viable arguments and critique the reasoning of others
6. Attend to precision

#1 WORD PROBLEM REWORK

ACTIVITY SUMMARY
Students will rework a math problem by changing one specific aspect of the problem. Some standard reworks are changing the numbers, the operation, the language, or the unit.

TIME: 45-minute lesson when introduced, 15 – 45 minutes when revisited

ACTIVITY IN ACTION
1. Students do the "Original Problem" as a Do Now or Warm-up activity.
2. Teacher goes over the "Original Problem" by teaching how to solve the problem.
3. Students work independently or in collaborative groups to rework the "Original Problem."
4. Students solve their reworked problems on a separate sheet.
5. Students exchange their newly reworked problem with a classmate. Each solving the others problem in the space provided.
6. Students explain to each other how they solved the others problem referring to the solution from steps 2 and 3.
7. Students can write about or verbally explain how they solved the problem and/or their rationale for the choices they provided.

ASSESSMENT
- Can the student solve the "Reworked" problem correctly?
- What strategies did students use to solve the "Reworked" problem?
- Does the "Reworked" problem make sense?

EXTENSIONS
- Math Centers: Have students rotate from one type of rework to another. For example, Table 1 will Change the Numbers, Table 2 will Change the Story, Table 3 will Change the Language, and Table 4 will Change the Operation. Students work at each table for about 10 minutes, and then rotate to another to do another rework.
- Problem of the Week: Have a Problem of the Week and do a different rework of that problem daily.
- Make a Booklet of Reworked Problems: This can be a great study tool, resource and a way for teachers and students to track progress over time.

FAQ
Q: Do I always have to use multiple-choice questions?
A: No, using multiple-choice questions are just one option and it has specific pros and cons. Using multiple-choices mimic the kind of questions that students will see on standardized exams. Using questions without multiple-choices or by removing the multiple-choices from a question increases the probability of getting more than four different answers. But, by using a question without the multiple-choices gives you a clearer understanding of how student might answer on constructed response items and gives greater insight into student misconceptions.

Fostering Test-Savvy Students

TEST-SAVVY PRINCIPLES

To become test-savvy, students need to know and understand three fundamental things: 1) the math content and how their understanding of those concepts might be assessed; 2) the mechanics and procedures of the test; and 3) their own personal strengths and challenges.

Fundamental Principles of Test-Savvy Test-Takers	
Principles	Test-Savvy Skills
1. Knows and understands grade-level math concepts and how those concepts might be assessed	1. Manipulates mathematical ideas as applied to real-world contexts 2. Generates their own problems and solutions 3. Discusses/critiques solutions 4. Identifies common misconceptions related to concepts 5. Understands how math terms are related and relate terms to other math concepts
2. Knows and understands test mechanics and procedures	6. Identifies/categorizes question types 7. Develops visual memory of the exam format 8. Develops the ability to skip around effectively, when needed
3. Knows and understands his/her personal strengths and challenges	9. Is self-reflective, critical of work 10. Seeks out, identifies, explains, and replicates errors as tools for learning 11. Analyzes data and identifies personal trends 12. Perseveres, is flexible even when questions are challenging, and has alternative strategies

As a part of any effective, research-based mathematics program, students should **know and understand grade-level math concepts and how those concepts might be assessed.** Opportunities to build (apply), test (analyze and evaluate) and enhance their own content knowledge (create) must be ritualized, and used on a consistent basis. In order to accomplish this, students must be afforded opportunities to Manipulates mathematical ideas as applied to real-world contexts and to generate their own problems while discussing and critiquing their solutions and the solutions of others. Students need to see and discuss misconceptions and see the identification of those misconceptions as pathways to clarity.

Test-savvy test-takers can identify the mathematical concepts behind a question. Test-savvy test-takers consciously tap into their prior knowledge to help them solve problems. Test-savvy test-takers can recognize specific concepts in a variety of forms. Test-savvy test-takers are able to determine when an algorithm is needed or if simply understanding the concept will help them see the answer. Test-savvy test-takers are able to identify distractors (incorrect answers based upon common errors) and expect specific ones. Test-savvy test-takers have a general understanding of the kind of problems that will be on the exam.

Standardized exams are generally used by most stakeholders to help determine promotion, placement in the next grade level, and to show student progress. While this belief is not new, it has been further entrenched due to No Child Left Behind (NCLB) mandated requirements. Schools, districts and states have to show annual yearly progress (AYP) via standardized test scores. Everyone takes these exams seriously and cannot afford not to. The consequences of not meeting AYP can be severe, ranging from external monitoring, reduction of specific federal funds, school restructuring and closure. NCLB aims that by 2014 all students will be at or above grade level. State-mandated standardized math exams happen once per year due in part to cost, timing constraints, and the need to quickly, yet unobtrusively gather data about student progress. It is imperative that students **know and understand test mechanics and procedures.**

Additionally, students must be a part of the assessment process, **knowing and understanding his/her personal strengths and challenges.** Data is driving how schools operate and organize themselves and how teachers instruct. However, very few students can articulate their own strengths or areas of challenge when it comes to math. At best, their responses generally add up to, "I know my times tables…most of them anyway." Students need to know, specifically which concepts they do know, how they mastered those concepts and which ones are giving them trouble.

We have one huge motivating factor on our side as educators – human beings are innately curious and self-centered. Life is about finding things out and figuring out how we relate to the world around us. We are questioning beings who ponder our place in the world and like to examine how we measure up. By teaching students how to be more self-reflective, how to search for and seek out errors in order to learn and how to analyze data, one enables students how to recognize their personalized strengths and areas of challenge. Please note, while some see the words challenge and weakness as interchangeable, they come from different belief systems that influence how one learns and teaches. A challenge is exciting, is faceable, and can be overcome. A weakness is perceived as innate, defeating, defining, and confining.

HOW STUDENTS LEARN TO BECOME BETTER TEST TAKERS

While every child can achieve, every child will not show their highest levels of achievement or understandings on a standardized exam, on a given day, at a given time. Every child will not achieve according to grade or age level expectations. Achievement is a personal and internal matter that is impacted by a multitude of variables ranging from known and unknown brain functioning, developmental levels, and environmental factors. It is within this context that we have to teach our students how to maximize their test scores, given their current levels of understanding.

Students learn to become better test takers by…	How is this actualized by teachers?
• reducing test anxiety	Incorporate strategies that build student confidence and stamina.
• understanding what they are doing and why they are doing it	Provide opportunities to create and discuss ideas.
• being reflective and aware of their own thinking	Evaluate the work of others, and by identifying their mistakes. Making mistakes on purpose and explaining the rationale behind the mistake.
• internalizing and accepting the process	Use student generated problems that model test questions.

The strategies outlined in *Test-Savvy Math: Fostering Thinking and Reasoning into the Test-Prep Process* can help your students to become better, more confident test-takers. Test-savviness helps students develop a "can-do" attitude about facing challenges on standardized exams and in life by preparing students to think and reason by tapping into prior knowledge, even when they are nervous and fearful.

GENERAL TRENDS OF STANDARDIZED EXAMS AND IMPLICATIONS FOR INSTRUCTION

The chart below outlines some general commonalities as related to the mechanics, procedures, and question items on standardized exams across the nation and the impact they have on instruction and student learning.

General Commonalities	Implications for Instruction
AYP for each student is determined by an approved (or pending approval) formula by each state.	Students need to know how exams are scored in their state.
Exams are **timed**. Even states that allow unlimited timing recommend a general time frame for students to complete the exams.	Students have to know how to use their time effectively.
Exams have **more than one section** and take **more than one day**.	Students have to have stamina and endurance.
Students are encouraged to **show their work** in the test booklets.	Students have to internalize the process of showing their work.
Specific **tools and manipulatives** are used.	Students must use tools and manipultives throughout the school year.
Most exams have **multiple-choice and constructed response** sections.	Students need to know the point value of each item on the exam and how they are scored.
Specific procedures for taking the exams.	Students and teachers need to know the exam procedures before the day of the test.
Exam questions are **field tested**.	Test-makers are savvy and can predict how students will answer specific questions. Students need to know how to recognize the test-makers tricks and traps (distractors).
Exam questions have **varying degrees of difficulty** and often require **multiple-steps**.	Students need to be consistently exposed to problems that require multiple-steps. The mathematics necessary to solve the problem needs to be presented in new, unique, or unfamiliar situations. Additionally, students need exposure to and opportunities to try multiple strategies and math models that can show their critical thinking skills.
Exam questions often **combine more than one area of mathematics**.	Students have to be flexible in their thinking, and be able to see the mathematical connections across domains and with previous learning.

TESTING IN THE AGE OF THE COMMON CORE STATE STANDARDS

"What all educational assessments have in common is the desire to reason from particular things students say, do, or make, to broader inferences about their knowledge and abilities."

– Mislevy, Almond, Lukas
A Brief Introduction to Evidence-Centered Design
Education Testing Service (ETS), 2003

Testing prior to the implementation of the CCSS assessments were norm-referenced (NRT), criterion-referenced tests (CRT) or a hybrid called "standard-referenced test," which is a CRT that has NRT elements. Assessments in the age of the CCSS use an evidence-centered design (ECD) model. The chart below defines and compares each model.

Norm Referenced (NRT)
• Compares and ranks students as to similar test takers (i.e., a cross section of 4th grade math students from across the nation).
• **Pros:** Provides an overview of how students are performing, when compared to others in similar groups nationwide. Easy to compare groups of student. Ready-made, validated.
• **Cons:** Not aligned to individual state standards. Does not test mastery of a topic or concept.
Criterion Referenced (CRT)
• Measures student knowledge and understanding of a specific body of knowledge (i.e. state grade-level math standards).
• **Pros:** Students are tested on states performance standards, instead of nationwide standards. Tests what the students have mastered.
• **Cons:** Needs to be developed, tested, and refined as standards are updated. Measures one standard at a time.
Evidence-Centered Design (ECD)
• Makes claims about what students know and can do based on evidence gathered via assessment tasks that are aligned to a specific set of standards.
• **Pros:** Provides a clear and more accurate picture about what students actually know, can do, and understand. Uses most up-to-date research on cognitive development and technology. Has the capability to be designed to test several standards in one item.
• **Cons:** The amount of time it takes to create exam questions, complete field-testing and the refinement of field-tested items.

A video produced by Smarter Balanced introducing evidence-centered design is located at: www.smarterbalanced.org/smarter-balanced-assessments/item-writing-and-review.

Unlike exam items developed using other assessment design models, evidence-centered design exam items are designed to measure multiple standards and/or domains within a single item and look to illicit evidence of understanding. The example below from the "Smarter Balanced Mathematics Item Specification Grades 3 – 5" models the difference between previously designed exam items (Item A) and exam items using an evidence-centered design model (Item B).

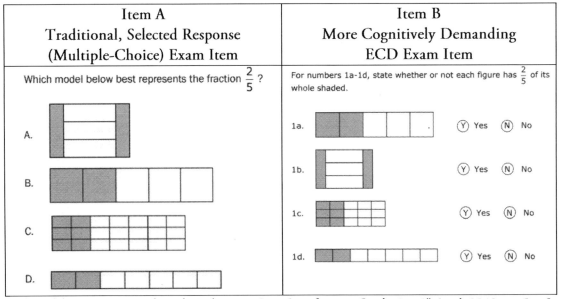

Adapted from "Smarter Balanced Mathematics Item Specification Grades 3 – 5" April, 2012, p. 5 – 6

For Item A, most students would select B, but we cannot be clear as to their reasoning. Smarter Balanced points out that many students would select option B, because it looks like a representation that students are familiar with. This item cannot produce sufficient evidence to make an accurate claim about how well a student understands fractions.

Item B requires greater evaluation and understanding of the concepts embodied by the task. This reworked problem now has 16 possible answers, thus significantly reducing a students ability to make an educated guess. This item does allow a claim to be made about how well a student knows and understands fractional amounts and how fractional amounts can be represented. Advances in technology allow for quick scoring of this item and assigning points based upon a rubric.

Scoring Rubric

Responses to this item will receive 0-2 points, based upon the following:

2 points: YNYN The student has a solid understanding of 2/5 as well as an equivalent form of 2/5.

1 point: YNNN, YYNN, YYYN The student has only a basic understanding of 2/5. Either the student doesn't recognize an equivalent fraction for 2/5 or doesn't understand that all 5 parts must be equal-sized in figure 1b.

0 points: YYYY, YNNY, NNNN, NNYY, NYYN, NYNN, NYYY, NYNN, NNNN, NYNY, NNYN, NNNY The student demonstrates inconsistent understanding of 2/5 or answers "Y" to figure 1d, clearly showing a misunderstanding of what 2/5 means. Figure 1d is considered a "disqualifier" and an answer of "Y" to this part of the item would cancel out any other correct responses as "guesses" on the part of the student.

Adapted from "Smarter Balanced Mathematics Item Specification Grades 3 – 5" April, 2012, p. 7

EVIDENCED-CENTERED DESIGN IMPACT ON INSTRUCTION

"Evidence-Centered Design supports the development of assessment tasks that address the Standards for Mathematical Practice. Thus, the kind of mathematics instruction called for in the CCSSM—engaging students in work that helps them develop mathematical habits of mind—can be reflected in powerful ways in the assessment system. Teachers will likely continue to "teach to the test," but, if the tests are designed in ways that reflect the standards (including the Standards for Mathematical Practice), then we will have together created assessment instruments that make teaching to the test a worthy undertaking for students and teachers."

– The Charles A. Dana Center at the University of Texas at Austin and Agile Mind, Inc.
www.ccsstoolbox.com/parcc/PARCCPrototype_main.html

When thinking about preparing our students for the kinds of assessments and challenges that they will face in the 21st Century, educators have to also be savvy about evidenced-centered design. Outlined below are five major things that educators need to know and understand about the evidence-centered design assessment model as it pertains to the CCSSM.

Educators need to understand and know:

1. **The principles and implementation structures upon which assessments are being designed by each assessment consortium.** The CCSS aligned assessments that are being produced and field tested look drastically different than anything previously seen at the 3 thru 8 grade levels. Both consortiums are being proactive about declaring the structures and formats of exam items. Both consortiums have similar items and task types. They are as follows:
   - Selected-response items (multiple-choice)
   - Technology-enhanced items (online, interactive, digital)
   - Constructed-response items (short answer or extended response)
   - Performance tasks (authentic task)

2. **The evidence-centered design claims for the assessment consortium that their state is a part of.** The claims of the assessments being produced are driven by the CCSS key instructional shifts of 1) focus, 2) coherence, and 3) rigor. These shifts are the foundation for the claims and underpin the assessment targets. Claims are the "big ideas" that cross grade levels

and domains. The claims drive the kind of evidence that will be collected, and subsequently, the kind of exam items that will be produced. For your convenience, the claims for Smarter Balanced and PARCC are charted in the Appendix (p. 131).

Introduction to Evidence-Centered Design by Smarter Balanced, June 2012

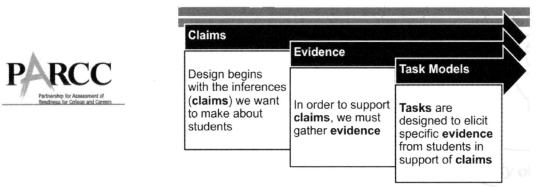

New Directions in Assessment: The PARCC Prototype Project, April 2012
www.utdanacenter.org/mathtoolkit/downloads/presentations/ncsm/hull-seeley-arrington-parcc-prototyping-ncsm-2012.pdf

3. **The assessment targets for each grade-level and their expected depth of knowledge (DOK) level.** Each claim is aligned to a set of assessment targets outlined by each consortium. An assessment target specifies the parameters of the content and establishes a cognitive demand level (depth of knowledge – DOK) that exam items must meet. Assessment targets are derived from the CCSSM and the Math Progressions. The web address to the Progressions and other valuable resources are listed in the Appendix (p. 130).

4. **Have an explicit understanding of what sufficient evidence looks like for each assessment target.** The communication of what students understand and know is at the heart of assessment items. ECD models craft items that aim to produce evidence in relationship to claims. Teachers must ensure that what is being taught and how it is being taught will render the kinds of evidence that align with the CCSS and the ECD claims, assessment targets, and evidence.

Examining an Item Through the Lens of Evidence-Centered Design

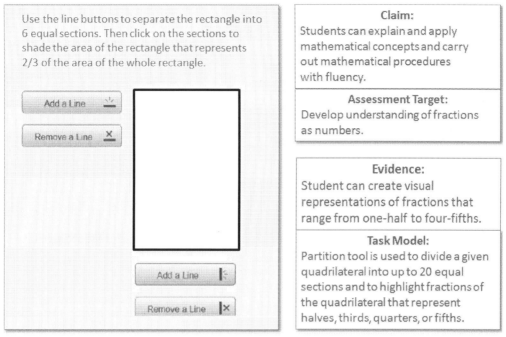

Introduction to Evidence-Centered Design by Smarter Balanced, June 2012

5. **Have an in depth understanding of each domain in the CCSS, the Mathematical Practices, and how the next generation of assessments will intertwine multiple standards, domains, and the Mathematical Practices into single exam items.** This is a major transition for many teachers who may be accustomed to teaching topics in isolation for coverage and/or exposure, opposed to depth and deep conceptual understanding. The tasks at Illustrative Mathematics (www.illustrativemathematics.org) exemplify the connected nature of mathematical concepts and domains.

HOW TEST-SAVVY MATH ADDRESSES THE RIGORS OF AN EVIDENCE-CENTERED DESIGN MODEL FOR THE CCSS

The research-based activities in *Test-Savvy Math: Fostering Thinking and Reasoning into the Test-Prep Process* were designed, tested, and enhanced (as needed) to provide teachers with structures that raise the cognitive demand of traditional test-prep experiences. The strategies outlined expect and require students to question, represent, and justify their thinking in a variety of ways and are grounded in the Mathematical Practices. Furthermore, activities suggest guiding questions and provide assessment opportunities to support teachers in consistently looking for evidence of how students apply the mathematics that they know and understand.

Getting Started

BECOMING A TEST-SAVVY TEACHER

Teaching is a craft that requires continual refinement via deliberate practice, study, reflection, and dedication. Teachers have to continuously filter information, everything from new research-based practices to how new groups of students react to a lesson that worked well with the previous years' students. The activities in *Test-Savvy Math: Fostering Thinking and Reasoning into the Test-Prep Process* require teachers to do the following…

- Make your students your partners in the educational process by building a math environment where rich discourse is expected, structured, nurtured, and students have a hand in developing content for the classroom.
- Use multiple data points to drive decisions about how to organize students and target topics for instruction.
- Commit to consistently using one or more test-savvy strategies and documenting student growth.
- Be patient with yourself and the discomfort that comes with trying something different.

THE FIRST STEPS

Preparation is the key to having a successful lesson, so before you implement…
- Review the *Test-Savvy Getting Started Organizer* located in the Appendix (p. 123). The organizer helps you focus on how, what, when, and why you are implementing a test-savvy strategy.
- Based on your student data, decide on a math concept or skill to target.
- Review the list of activities on pages 18 – 19 and select one that addresses the test-savvy skills you aim to build.
- Prepare handouts for students using activity templates.
- If you are unsure about the flow of the activity, try it out with a colleague first.
- Do the problems for the activity prior to implementation.
- Decide how you are going to group students and establish classroom norms for working together.
- Commit to revisiting the activity at least 3 more times.

FINDING PROBLEMS TO USE

You can get problems from…

- Text book resources.
- Curriculum materials that have "Test-Prep" sections.
- Commercial test-prep resources that identify the specific standards being addressed and provide numerous examples.
- District or state resources that might have sample exams and student sample responses.
- Online resources such as NEAP, Illustrative Mathematics or states such as New York, Florida or Massachusetts that have released exam items from previous years.
- Actual student work samples that you have collected from students. For privacy purposes, it is best to remove student names.

IMPLEMENTING A TEST-SAVVY STRATEGY

Once you are ready to begin…

- Explain the task to your students and why you are doing it.
- Model the activity for your students.
- Explain the standard(s) addressed.
- Share the data with students about why this concept, procedure or skill is being revisited.
- Tell students that they are expected to voice their understandings and confusions.
- Tell students that they will help each other learn by questioning one another.
- Tell students that they are expected to note what is really "fuzzy" or confusing to them.

GATHERING DATA & DOCUMENTING PROGRESS

In the Appendix you will find resources to help you document and track student growth and progress. Resources include…

- An informal *Test-Savvy Survey* and instructions for implementation, which measures where a student falls on a point scale of "not test-savvy" to "test-savvy".
- The *Test-Savvy Teacher Data Tracking Sheet* can be used to record an activity, dates implemented, pre/post activity data, and teacher reflection on each time the activity was implemented.

ACTIVELY INCORPORATE THE MATHEMATICAL PRACTICES

The Mathematical Practices (MP) embody how we show our understanding of, communicate, reason, model, and see the structure in mathematics. These practices come to life as students engage in the strategies outlined in *Test-Savvy Math: Fostering Thinking and Reasoning into the Test-Prep Process*. To make the practices more explicit for students, teachers could do the following…

- During lessons ask higher order thinking questions that allow students to reflect on the Mathematical Practices. For example, ask students to share how they persevered in solving a problem (MP #1) or have students model and explain their thinking using various math models (MP #3, MP #4).
- Highlight one Mathematical Practice at the start of a lesson and ask students to keep track of how many times they are enacting that practice during the course of the lesson.

IDEAS FOR LEAD TEACHERS, COACHES & ADMINISTRATORS

Some ways that *Test-Savvy Math: Fostering Thinking and Reasoning into the Test-Prep Process* can be used to build teacher comfort level and ensure consistent usage is by scheduling one or more of the following activities…

- Set up a lab site where an activity is demonstrated.
- During planning sessions discuss identified student needs and activities from *Test-Savvy Math: Fostering Thinking and Reasoning into the Test-Prep Process* that might be used to address those needs.
- Discuss the student samples focusing on one or more of the discussion points.
- Select three to five strategies to pilot during the course of one school year. Set times, dates and debriefing sessions to discuss student progress as evidenced by student work samples.

IDEAS FOR CURRICULUM COORDINATORS AND DISTRICTS

Test-Savvy Math: Fostering Thinking and Reasoning into the Test-Prep Process can be used as part of a district-wide initiative to improve student thinking and reasoning by incorporating one or more of the following activities…

- Videotape classroom lessons of the strategies in action and make them available on the district website for teachers to review.
- Document teacher use of specific strategies and track student progress on targeted concepts or skills across the district.

- Have a district-wide workshop to introduce and model the strategies for teachers, coaches, and administrators.
- Select ten strategies to pilot during the course of one school year. Have teachers select one of the ten strategies to enact. Set up collaborative reflection circle strategy groups where teachers can look at student work, discuss data, and how they have adapted the specific strategy that they are piloting to better meet the needs of their students.

Test-Savvy Math: Fostering Thinking and Reasoning into the Test-Prep Process will encourage you to revisit test-prep in another way and inspire your creativity to develop your own test-savvy activities. This is a journey our students need us to take. The level of critical thinking that students experience via these activities will make your efforts both rewarding and worthwhile.

Quick Glance

TEST-SAVVY ACTIVITIES & SKILLS

TEST-SAVVY ACTIVITIES	1 Manipulates mathematical ideas as applied to real-world contexts	2 Generates their own problems & solutions	3 Discusses/critiques solutions	4 Identifies common misconceptions related to concepts	5 Understands how math terms are related and relate terms to other math concepts
1. Work Problem Rework	✓	✓	✓	✓	✓
2. Rate My Work	✓	✓	✓	✓	✓
3. Find and Fix My Error	✓	✓	✓	✓	✓
4. Word Problem Carousel	✓	✓	✓		✓
5. Question Category			✓	✓	✓
6. I Review		✓	✓	✓	
7. Two Arguments	✓		✓	✓	✓
8. Collaborative Explanation	✓	✓	✓	✓	✓
9. Concept Square	✓		✓		✓
10. Frayer Model Problem Solving	✓	✓	✓		✓
11. Rally Round the Problem	✓	✓	✓		✓
12. Match the Math Picture	✓	✓	✓	✓	
13. Show Me in Many Ways	✓	✓	✓	✓	
14. Visual Verbal Word Association	✓	✓	✓	✓	✓
15. Representing the Operation	✓	✓	✓	✓	
16. Evaluating the Choices	✓	✓	✓	✓	
17. Match the Choices	✓	✓	✓	✓	
18. What is the Question?	✓	✓	✓		
19. What are the Choices?	✓	✓	✓	✓	
20. Multiple-Choice in Minutes	✓	✓	✓	✓	
21. Sunflower Word Riddle					✓
22. Vocabulary Tic Tac Toe	✓	✓	✓		✓
23. Word Clusters	✓	✓	✓		✓
24. School Yard Hand Game	✓	✓	✓		✓
25. Mystery Word	✓	✓	✓		✓

Activities in *Test-Savvy Math: Fostering Thinking and Reasoning into the Test-Prep Process* address specific test-savvy skills. The chart below provides an easy overview and reference of all skills addressed[1].

6	7	8	9	10	11	12
Identify/ categorize question types	Develops visual memory of the exam format	Develops the ability to skip around effectively, when needed	Is self-reflective, critical of work	Seeks out, identifies, explains and replicates errors as tools for learning	Analyzes data and identifies personal trends	Perseveres, is flexible even when questions are challenging, and has alternative strategies
	✓		✓	✓	✓	✓
	✓		✓	✓	✓	✓
	✓		✓	✓	✓	✓
✓	✓		✓	✓		✓
✓	✓		✓		✓	
✓	✓		✓	✓	✓	✓
✓			✓	✓		✓
	✓		✓		✓	✓
			✓			
	✓					✓
✓	✓					✓
			✓			✓
			✓			✓
			✓		✓	✓
	✓		✓	✓		✓
	✓		✓	✓		✓
✓	✓	✓				✓
	✓					✓
	✓		✓	✓		✓
✓	✓	✓	✓		✓	✓
			✓		✓	✓
						✓
						✓
						✓

[1] Please note that not all of the test-savvy skills listed in this chart are listed in each lesson, due to space constraints.
Test-Savvy Math By Christine King, © 2013 CKingEducation, Inc.

CCSS Mathematical Practices

The activities and student work samples in *Test-Savvy Math: Fostering Thinking and Reasoning into the Test-Prep Process* are grounded in the Mathematical Practices from the Common Core State Standards and can be used to help actualize them in the classroom.

1. **Make sense of problems and persevere in solving them.**
   - Explaining the meaning of a problem
   - Analyze givens, constraints, relationships, and goals
   - Make conjectures about the form and meaning of the solution and plan a solution pathway rather than simply jumping into a solution attempt
   - Evaluate their progress and change course if necessary

2. **Reason abstractly and quantitatively.**
   - Make sense of quantities and their relationships in problem situations.
   - Decontextualize—to abstract a given situation and represent it symbolically and manipulate the representing symbols as if they have a life of their own.
   - Contextualize, to pause as needed during the manipulation process in order to probe into the referents for the symbols involved.
   - Creating a coherent representation of the problem at hand; considering the units involved; attending to the meaning of quantities, not just how to compute them; and knowing and flexibly using different properties of operations and objects.

3. **Construct viable arguments and critique the reasoning of others.**
   - Understand and use stated assumptions, definitions, and previously established results in constructing arguments.
   - Make conjectures and build a logical progression of statements to explore the truth of their conjectures.
   - Analyze situations by breaking them into cases, and can recognize and use counterexamples.
   - Justify their conclusions, communicate them to others, and respond to the arguments of others.
   - Reason inductively about data, making plausible arguments that take into account the context from which the data arose.
   - Compare the effectiveness of two plausible arguments, distinguish correct logic or reasoning from that which is flawed, and—if there is a flaw in an argument—explain what it is.

4. Model with mathematics.
- Apply the mathematics they know to solve problems arising in everyday life, society, and the workplace.
- Apply what they know and are comfortable making assumptions and approximations to simplify a complicated situation, but realize that these may need revision later.
- Identify important quantities in a practical situation and map their relationships using such tools as diagrams, two-way tables, graphs, flowcharts and formulas.
- Analyze relationships mathematically to draw conclusions.
- Interpret mathematical results in the context of the situation and reflect on whether the results make sense

5. Use appropriate tools strategically.
- Consider the available tools when solving a mathematical problem.
- Detect possible errors by strategically using estimation and other mathematical knowledge
- When making mathematical models, they know that technology can enable them to visualize the results of varying assumptions, explore consequences, and compare predictions with data.
- Use technological tools to explore and deepen their understanding of concepts

6. Attend to precision.
- Mathematically proficient students try to communicate precisely to others.
- Use clear definitions in discussion with others and in their own reasoning.
- State the meaning of the symbols they choose, including using the equal sign consistently and appropriately.
- Careful about specifying units of measure, and labeling axes to clarify the correspondence with quantities in a problem.
- They calculate accurately and efficiently, express numerical answers with a degree of precision appropriate for the problem context.

7. Look for and make use of structure.
- Mathematically proficient students look closely to discern a pattern or structure.
- Step back for an overview and can shift perspective.
- See complicated things as single objects or composed of several objects.

8. Look for and express regularity in repeated reasoning.
- Mathematically proficient students notice if calculations are repeated, and look both for general methods and for shortcuts.
- As they work to solve a problem, mathematically proficient students maintain oversight of the process, while attending to the details.
- They continually evaluate the reasonableness of their intermediate results.

NCTM Process Standards

The activities and student work samples in *Test-Savvy Math: Fostering Thinking and Reasoning into the Test-Prep Process* are linked to the NCTM Process Standards and can be incorporated into any instructional program. Teachers are encouraged to reflect on how these activities promote reasoning, communication, and modeling of mathematical thinking.

1. **Problem Solving:**
    Instructional programs should enable all students to…
    - Build new mathematical knowledge through open-ended questions and more-extended exploration;
    - Allow students to recognize and choose a variety of appropriate strategies to solve problems;
    - Think & Discuss and Share & Summarize to allow students to reflect on their own and other strategies for solving problems.

2. **Reasoning & Proof:**
    Instructional programs should enable all students to…
    - Recognize and create conjectures based on patterns they observe;
    - Investigate math conjectures and prove that in all cases they are true or that one counterexample shows that it is not true;
    - Explain and justify their solutions.

3. **Communication:**
    Instructional programs should enable all students to…
    - Organize and consolidate their mathematical thinking in written and verbal communication;
    - Communicate their mathematical thinking clearly to peers, teachers, and others;
    - Use mathematical vocabulary to express mathematical ideas precisely.

4. **Connections:**
    Instructional programs should enable all students to…
    - Understand that mathematical ideas are interconnected and that they build and support each other;
    - Recognize and apply connections to other contents;
    - Solve real world problems with mathematical connections.

5. **Representation:**
    Instructional programs should enable all students to…
    - Emphasize a variety of mathematical representations including written descriptions, diagrams, equations, graphs, pictures, and tables;
    - Select, apply, and translate among mathematical representations to solve problems;
    - Model real-life situations.

Section 1

YEAR-LONG TEST-SAVVY ACTIVITIES

"The mathematics students need to learn today is not the same mathematics that their parents and grandparents needed to learn. When today's students become adults, they will face new demands for mathematical proficiency that school mathematics should attempt to anticipate. Moreover, mathematics is a realm no longer restricted to a select few. All young Americans must learn to think mathematically, and they must think mathematically to learn."

— *Adding It Up*
National Research Council, 2001

The activities detailed in Section 1 adhere to the belief that providing structured learning environments, where students are allowed and expected to apply their knowledge, analyze what is presented, evaluate their own understandings, and create problems as a mechanism of internalizing information yields students who are better able to think critically about problems on standardized exams and in life. When used consistently, these strategies build habits of mind that promote a mental shift that expands how students look at and take ownership of problems on standardized exams.

PONDER THIS...

- Learning is enhanced if students are asked to do the following:
    1. State the information in their own words.
    2. Give examples of it.
    3. Recognized in various guises and circumstances.
    4. See connections between it and other facts or ideas.
    5. Make use of it in various ways.
    6. Foresee some of its consequences.
    7. State its opposite or converse (John Holt, 1967, Mel Siberman, 1996, p. 3).

- Supporting students to become aware of and engaged in their own learning will serve them well in all learning endeavors (Donovan & Bransford, 2005, p. 12).

- Students need to know what learning targets they are responsible for mastering and at what level. Students who can identify what they are learning significantly outscore those who cannot (Marzano, 2005, Chappuis, 2005).

LEARNING OBJECTIVE
Students will be able to solve problems similar to the "Original Problem."
GUIDING QUESTIONS
• Do your numbers make sense given the context/situation? Why? • How does the problem change? • How do your changes affect the solution?
MATERIALS
• Template: Word Problem Rework • A multiple-choice question
TEST-SAVVY SKILLS
• Manipulates mathematical ideas as applied to real-world contexts • Generates their own problems & solutions • Discusses/critiques solutions • Identifies common misconceptions related to concepts • Develops visual memory of the exam format • Is self-reflective, critical of work • Seeks out, identifies, explains, and replicates errors as tools for learning • Perseveres, is flexible even when questions are challenging, and has alternative strategies
MATHEMATICAL PRACTICES
1 Make sense of problems and persevere in solving them
2 Reason abstractly and quantitatively
3 Construct viable arguments and critique the reasoning of others
6 Attend to precision

#1 WORD PROBLEM REWORK

ACTIVITY SUMMARY

Students will rework a math problem by changing one specific aspect of the problem. Some standard reworks are changing the numbers, the operation, the language or the unit.

TIME: 45-minute lesson when introduced, 15 – 45 minutes when revisited

ACTIVITY IN ACTION

1. Students do the "Original Problem" as a Do Now or Warm-up activity.
2. Teacher goes over the "Original Problem" by teaching how to solve the problem.
3. Students work independently or in collaborative groups to rework the "Original Problem."
4. Students solve their reworked problems on a separate sheet.
5. Students exchange their newly reworked problem with a classmate. Each solving the others problem in the space provided.
6. Students explain to each other how they solved the others problem referring to the solution from steps 2 and 3.
7. Students can write about or verbally explain how they solved the problem and/or their rationale for the choices they provided.

ASSESSMENT

- Can the student solve the "Reworked" problem correctly?
- What strategies did students use to solve the "Reworked" problem?
- Does the "Reworked" problem make sense?

EXTENSIONS

- Math Centers: Have students rotate from one type of rework to another. For example, Group 1 will Change the Numbers, Group 2 will Change the Story, Group 3 will Change the Language, and Group 4 will Change the Operation. Students work at each table for about 10 minutes, and then rotate to do another rework.
- Problem of the Week: Have a Problem of the Week and do a different rework of that problem daily.
- Make a Booklet of Reworked Problems: This can be a great study tool and a way for teachers and students to track progress over time.

FAQ

Q: Do I always have to use multiple-choice questions?

A: No, using multiple-choice questions are just one option and it has specific pros and cons. Using multiple-choices mimic the kind of questions that students will see on standardized exams. Using questions without multiple-choices or by removing the multiple-choices from a question increases the probability of getting more than four different answers. But, by using a question without the multiple-choices gives you a clearer understanding of how students might answer constructed response items and give greater insight into student misconceptions.

DIFFERENT TYPES OF WORD PROBLEM REWORKS

Original Word Problem*:

3 Ray bought 3 notebooks. Each notebook contained 90 sheets of paper. How many sheets of paper did Ray buy in all?

- A 30
- B 90
- C 180
- D 270

Change the Numbers, Same Words
Ray bought 5 notebooks. Each notebook contained 125 sheets of paper.
How many sheets of paper did Ray buy in all?

Change the Operation Needed
Ray had 90 sheets of paper. Each notebook contained 45 sheets of paper.
How many notebooks did Ray buy in all?
Or
Ray bought 3 notebooks. Ray had 270 sheets of paper in total.
How many sheets of paper were in each notebook?

Same Numbers, Same Operations, Write a Different Story
Jose had 90 baseball cards. His father said that if he got all A's on this next report card he would buy him triple that amount. How many baseball cards would Jose's father buy him if he got all A's on his next report card?

Same Numbers, Same Operations, Change the Language
Ray purchased 3 composition books. Each composition book had 90 pieces of paper.
How many pieces of paper did Ray purchase in total?

Same Numbers Represented Differently
Ray bought three notebooks. Each notebook contained ninety sheets of paper.
How many sheets of paper did Ray buy in all?
Or
Ray bought 2 notebooks and one more. Each notebook contained 50 blue and 40 yellow sheets of paper. How many sheets of paper did Ray buy in all?

Same Story, Change the Unit
Ray bought 3 loaves of bread. Each loaf of bread contained 90 slices of bread.
How many slices of bread did Ray buy in all?

Ask for Three Problem-Solving Strategies
- Draw a Picture
- Act It Out
- Use Logic

Write Equations to Express Answers
- 3 x 90 = 270
- 90 + 90 + 90 = 270

*The "Original Word Problem" from the New York State Department of Education Grade 4 Sample Test, 2005

NAME: _____   DATE: _____

Sample WORD PROBLEM REWORK

ORIGINAL PROBLEM:
Jamie wanted to go the movies with her friend. She had $7.00 saved up and her friend had $8.00. Movie tickets cost $6.50 each, but are 10% off on Tuesdays. How much money would they have left to spend on popcorn and drinks, if they went to the movies on Tuesday?

A) $1.30

B) $3.30

C) $11.70

D) $15.00

REWORK #1: Change the Numbers, Same Story

Jamie wanted to go the movies with her friend. She had $5.00 saved up and her friend had $10.00. Movie tickets cost $5.00 each, but are 15% off on Tuesdays. How much money would they have left to spend on popcorn and drinks, if they went to the movies on Tuesday?

A) $4.25

B) $6.50

C) $10.00

D) $15.00

REWORK #2: Change the Story, Same Numbers

At a garage sale a book that I wanted cost $7.00, another cost $8.00, and the last book that I wanted cost $6.50. The lady in charge said that she would give me a 10% discount, if I bought all the books. How much money would I save with a 10% discount?

A) $2.15

B) $19.35

C) $21.50

D) $23.65

In Our Culture of Testing…Can Creativity Flourish?

Every year I watch the same cycle…either educators who worry about testing from day one or the ones who worry about testing six weeks prior to the date of THE TEST. Either way the results are the same…educators worry about standardized testing. I was reading a funny, well thought out story about standardized testing, *Testing Miss Malarkey*. The story is presented from the point-of-view of the students, the actual test-takers. They mention how the adults and even their parents started to act strange and school as they had known it…changed because of THE TEST. In art class, they made posters about how to fill-in the circles on the test in a "good, clean, neat and nice" fashion. In gym class, they began to practice yoga to prepare their "minds and bodies." Parents started giving their kids power bars to build the brain. On the day of the actual test, sick, nauseated teachers overran the nurse's office. And strangely enough, after the test things returned to normal…leaving the students to conclude, "THE TEST really wasn't that important after all."

The fact is we do a disservice to our students and ourselves by negating THE TEST on the surface, while allowing our actions to show that we are deeply, DEEPLY vested in testing. Maybe it is because we do not have a better system. Maybe we are scared to enact a better system. Whatever the reason, if we accept standardized testing, either by conscious choice or by default, then we need to acknowledge it, accept it, **BUT allow for creativity and critical thinking despite it!**

Excerpt from post at "Test-Savvy Math" at http://testsavvymath.blogspot.com

LEARNING OBJECTIVE
Students will be able to evaluate the work of others and themselves using rubrics.
GUIDING QUESTIONS
• Why would you give that score? • How could this work be improved? • How is your own work similar or different from the work that you are evaluating?
MATERIALS
• Template: Rate My Work • a constructed response question • 2 to 4 graded work samples of the same question • a state testing rubric
TEST-SAVVY SKILLS
• Generates their own problems & solutions • Discusses/critiques solutions • Identifies common misconceptions related to concepts • Develops visual memory of the exam format • Is self-reflective, critical of work • Seeks out, identifies, explains, and replicates errors as tools for learning • Analyzes data and identifies personal trends • Perseveres, is flexible even when questions are challenging, and has alternative strategies
MATHEMATICAL PRACTICES
1 Make sense of problems and persevere in solving them 3 Construct viable arguments and critique the reasoning of others 6 Attend to precision

#2 RATE MY WORK

ACTIVITY SUMMARY
Students review several work samples of a specific problem that have been graded using a rubric and discuss how each work sample could be improved.

TIME: 45-minutes when introducing the activity, 15 – 30 minutes when revisited

ACTIVITY IN ACTION
1. Students work independently to complete the "Original Problem" as a Do Now or Warm-up activity.
2. Teacher collects papers, so students do not make corrections to their own papers.
3. Teacher shows students rubric and work samples. Students discuss and evaluate.
4. Teacher exchanges and redistributes student papers to peers.
5. Peers evaluate student work using rubric and give students a score.
6. Peers explain, verbally and/or in writing, how they arrived at the score and give advice as to how to improve their grade.
7. Peers return papers to classmates.
8. Students explain if they thought the score and feedback was accurate or helpful.

ASSESSMENT
- Were students able to effectively evaluate the work of others?
- Do the grades given by the peer match the grade that you would give? Note how the students showed their work and the language used in their explanations.

EXTENSIONS
- Have students work collaboratively to evaluate student work samples, but do not show the scores. At the end of the lesson, average the marks of all of the groups and compare the actual score that was given.
- Have students work collaboratively to revamp and raise the score of a student work sample
- Have students work independently or collaboratively to try to get a specific score (i.e. on a 4-point rubric, have some students try to get a 2). Note the discussion. Have students write about what they had to do or not do to achieve the specified score. Have another group grade the work to see if they attained their goal.
- Have students work independently to solve a problem, then before you show work samples, have them work in small homogenous collaborative groups to re-do the problem together. They can show their work to each other, and use all of their ideas in the re-do.

FAQ
Q: How do I get student samples?
A: Some commercial products are available (i.e. Exemplars), but some free online resources are available (PALM – Performance Assessment Links in Mathematics, NEAP, Mathematics Task Bank by the Albuquerque Public Schools). Also, check on your district or state website for sample tasks with student samples. You can also use actual student work by removing their identifying information or simply make up your own.

NAME: _____ DATE: _____

Sample RATE MY WORK

1. Solve the problem, independently. You have __5__ minutes.
2. Exchange your paper with a peer. Peers Name: __Helen__
3. Use a rubric to evaluate and score your peers paper.
4. Explain to your peer the score you gave him/her.
5. On the back of this sheet, explain if you thought your score was fair. How could you improve your mark?

Problem

(NAEP national performance results in Mathematics at grade 8: 2007, 26% had this item correct)

13. Sara was asked to draw a parallelogram. She drew the figure below.

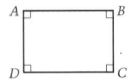

Is Sara's figure a parallelogram? Why or why not?

yes, Sara's figure is a parallelogram because it has four sides.

Score:	Peer Explanation of Score Given:
1	You received a score of 1 using a 0 to 3 point holistic rubric, because you did not fully explain why the figure was a parallelogram. If a polygon has 4 sides, then that means it is a quadrilateral, but not necessarily a parallelogram. You did not mention the pairs of parallel lines that the figure had...you needed to explain what a parallelogram was and you only began to explain one of the attributes of a quadrilateral.

Test-Savvy Math By Christine King, © 2013 CKingEducation, Inc.

#3 FIND AND FIX MY ERROR

LEARNING OBJECTIVE
Students will be able to identify and explain mathematical errors and offer alternative solution pathways and strategies.

GUIDING QUESTIONS
• Why do you think the student made that error?
• What could you do to avoid making a similar error?
• Why did you select that strategy?

MATERIALS
• Template: Find and Fix My Error
• Sample of student work that contains an error

TEST-SAVVY SKILLS
• Discusses/critiques solutions
• Identifies common misconceptions related to concepts
• Is self-reflective, critical of work
• Seeks out, identifies, explains, and replicates errors as tools for learning
• Analyzes data and identifies personal trends
• Perseveres, is flexible even when questions are challenging, and has alternative strategies

MATHEMATICAL PRACTICES	
1	Make sense of problems and persevere in solving them
2	Reason abstractly and quantitatively
3	Construct viable arguments and critique the reasoning of others
4	Model with mathematics
5	Use appropriate tools strategically
6	Attend to precision
7	Look for and make use of structure

ACTIVITY SUMMARY

Students work to identify an error that was made by another student on a "target problem." The target problem or problems have an error that reflects a common misconception made by many students.

TIME: 45 minutes for lesson

ACTIVITY IN ACTION

1. Teachers show/revisit various strategies that could be used for the kind of problem that the students are going to be presented.
2. Show the students a problem that contains an error.
3. Students identify the error(s).
4. Discuss and chart additional/alternative strategies that could be used to solve the problem.
5. Students recommend ways that the same error could be avoided by the student.
6. Share out and review the strategies and recommendations.

ASSESSMENT

- Can the students identify the errors?
- Can the students suggest additional/alternative strategies to solve the problems?

EXTENSIONS

- Math Centers: Develop centers where students can focus on a different area of mathematics, i.e. Algebra Find and Fix My Error Center, Geometry Find and Fix My Error Center, etc.
- Book of Strategies: Photograph samples of student strategies by math topic (i.e. strategies for area problems) and place in a book or binder for all students to access and reflect upon.

FAQ

Q: Should I have my students do the problem first?
A: No. If you are using data to determine the problem topic, then your students have already done this kind of problem and you know how they will perform. Tell the students from the beginning that this problem has an error, that way students who might have made a similar error are forewarned that this is incorrect.

Q: Can I use "target problems" from my own students?
A: Yes. Save samples of student work from previous years or borrow classwork from another teacher to get authentic student work. Make sure that you take off the name of the student whose sample you are using.

NAME: _____   DATE: _____

Sample FIND AND FIX MY ERROR

Directions:
1. The problem is incorrect. Read the problem.
2. Find the error.
3. Fix the error.
4. Explain the error that was made.
5. Use a different strategy to show the student how to do the problem correctly.
6. Tell the student how to avoid making that error in the future.

Target Problem:
(8th Grade Example from NYC Sample Exam 2005)

 Tracy's dog eats 8 ounces of dog food every day. How many pounds of dog food will her dog eat in 40 days?

Show your work.

```
    8 ounces
  x    7 days
  ─────────
    56 ounces a week
  x    40
  ─────────
   2240 lbs
```

Answer ___2240___ pounds

Explain the Error:

The student made a mistake when they multiplied 56 ounces x 40. They did 8 ounces x 7 days, which is 56 ounces of dog food for 1 week, so when they multiplied 56 ounces x 40 they were getting the answer for how many ounces of dog food Tracy's dog ate in 40 weeks, not 40 days.

Another mistake was that they changed the unit...ounces to pounds, but they did not do a conversion, they just changed the label.

Explain and Show an Additional Strategy:

The student could have used a ratio table to show the days, the ounces, and the pounds. I would have used this strategy, because I would see the relationship between the days, ounces and pounds. I saw that 1 day was 8 ounces or half-pound. If I multiply each row by 40 I would have 40 days, 320 ounces, and 20 pounds.

Days	1	2	4	40
Ounces	8	16	32	320
Pounds	1/2	1	2	20

Test-Savvy Math By Christine King, © 2013 CKingEducation, Inc.

LEARNING OBJECTIVE

Students will be able to create and solve grade level appropriate word problems.

GUIDING QUESTIONS

- Is this a realistic situation? Why?
- Why is the mathematics involved in this problem appropriate for your grade level?

MATERIALS

- sample problems
- different colored pens/pencils
- Word Problem Carousel

TEST-SAVVY SKILLS

- Manipulates mathematical ideas as applied to real-world contexts
- Generates their own problems & solutions
- Discusses/critiques solutions
- Understands how math terms are related and relate terms to other math concepts
- Develops visual memory of the exam format
- Is self-reflective, critical of work
- Seeks out, identifies, explains, and replicates errors as tools for learning
- Perseveres, is flexible even when questions are challenging, and has alternative strategies

MATHEMATICAL PRACTICES

1	Make sense of problems and persevere in solving them
2	Reason abstractly and quantitatively
6	Attend to precision
7	Look for and make use of structure
8	Look for and express repeated regularity in reasoning

#4 WORD PROBLEM CAROUSEL

ACTIVITY SUMMARY

Students work in groups no larger than four to create a word problem. Similar to a writing carousel

TIME: 30 – 45 minutes for lesson

ACTIVITY IN ACTION

1. Each group of students review sample problems similar to the ones you wish them to create.
2. Each student selects a different color pen/pencil.
3. The first student begins writing the first sentence in the word problem. This student is setting the stage or establishing the scenario for the problem.
4. The second student writes the second sentence in the word problem. This student is adding a related and relevant mathematical detail.
5. The third student can either write an additional relevant and related mathematical detail or they could write the question for the problem.
6. If a question was not written, then the fourth person writes the question. If a question was written, then the fourth person reads the question.
7. The group discusses and solves the problem.

ASSESSMENT

- Can the students solve the problems that they created?
- Are the problems generated grade-level appropriate?
- Can the students explain the relevance of their contribution to the overall problem?

EXTENSIONS

- Use problems created as homework, in Math Centers, as Warm-ups, or include in exams.
- Have students provide feedback to others in terms of their problems and solutions.
- Create a digital record of various problems that students can use for later reference.
- Give the students the first sentence of a word problem and have them build on that sentence.

FAQ

Q: Do I need to use different colored pens/pencils?
A: It helps. You do not need to use different colored pens/pencils per se, but it helps when you assess the student created questions and are able to look at what specific students contributed to the overall problem.

Q: What if students solve their own problems incorrectly?
A: It happens. This is a great way to develop a collection of incorrect problems for the whole class to revisit. It is important that students see the errors/misconceptions of others, as we are all subject to make mistakes, but awareness is a preventative measure that helps students be more reflective about their own work.

NAME: _____   DATE: _____

Sample WORD PROBLEM CAROUSEL

Multiple-choice Question

Statement #1	In 4 months Ms. Manning saved $822.00 for the new living room set that she wanted.
Statement #2	The set she wanted costs $998.00 at Bob's Discount Furniture Store.
Question	Which equation could Ms. Manning use to figure out how much more she will need to save before she can purchase the living room set?
Choice A	1000 − 800 = ___
Choice B	822 + ___ = 998
Choice C	998 − 822 + 4 = ___
Choice D	822 + 998 = ___

Constructed Response

Statement #1	While at the playground Malcolm and Jordan saw that each had three packs of nine Pokemon cards.
Statement #2	Jordan gave away 1 pack to his friend Terri.
Statement #3	Later that day Malcolm went to the store and bought another set just like the one that Jordan had given away.
Question	How many Pokemon cards did they each have?

*Please note: Each font variation represents a different students' contribution to the Collaborative Explanation.

Test-Savvy Math By Christine King, © 2013 CKingEducation, Inc.

LEARNING OBJECTIVE
Students will be able to identify, explain, and use the question categories to reflect on how challenging a problem will be for them.

GUIDING QUESTIONS
• How can knowing the question category help you solve the problem?
• What can you do if you realize that a particular question category is a challenge for you?

MATERIALS
• Template: Question Category
• questions representing the various types

TEST-SAVVY SKILLS
• Discusses/critiques solutions
• Identifies common misconceptions related to concepts
• Identifies/categorizes question types
• Understands how math terms are related and relate terms to other math concepts
• Develops visual memory of the exam format
• Is self-reflective, critical of work
• Analyzes data and identifies personal trends

MATHEMATICAL PRACTICES	
1	Make sense of problems and persevere in solving them
2	Reason abstractly and quantitatively
3	Construct viable arguments and critique the reasoning of others
4	Model with mathematics
5	Use appropriate tools strategically
6	Attend to precision
7	Look for and make use of structure

#5 QUESTION CATEGORY

ACTIVITY SUMMARY
Students identify the type of question (conceptual, procedural, visual spatial reasoning, use of tools or vocabulary), discuss ways to solve and note the types of distractors used.

TIME: 30 minutes when introducing the activity, 15 minutes when revisited

SET-UP
1. Gather problems representing the various problem types.
2. Arrange students into pairs or groups of 3 to 4 students.
3. Determine the problem categories for each pair or group.

ACTIVITY IN ACTION
1. Students are shown or reminded of the various question categories.
2. Student pairs are given a question and asked to identify the question categories and as a result the implications for solving the problem, including how long it should take.
3. Students share their analysis of the question with the whole class.

ASSESSMENT
- Can the students identify the problem category?
- Can the students explain how best to solve this type of problem?

EXTENSIONS
- Make a commercial. Have students make a one-minute commercial about the various questions categories by domain or by standard. In the commercial students might discuss some ways to solve questions in that category.
- Make a database or book of questions by category and domain. Have students work to contribute to this database or book by either finding problems or making up their own.
- Play a Jeopardy-like game where the questions represent the various problem types. Students gain points by identifying the problem category and them solving the problem.

FAQ
Q: Can some problems fit into more than one category?
A: Yes. Many problems clearly fit into one category or another, but some can fit into two or three categories. For example, the following problem can be considered both conceptual and procedural.

"Maria was asked to simplify the expression $3x + 7x + 5$. She wrote 15. Show Mary how to simplify the expression and explain why her answer is incorrect using a real-life example."

UNDERSTANDING QUESTION CATEGORIES

QUESTION CATEGORY	EXAMPLE
Conceptual Questions • Nothing to calculate. If you understand the concept, then you can see the solution and/or the relationships.	Imani wrote the expression 45 + 13 and asked Janine to figure it out. Janine re-wrote the expression as: $(40 + 10) + (5 + 3)$ Imani is not sure if Janine's way is correct. Explain to Imani if Janine's way will give the sum to 45 + 13.
Procedural Questions • Require calculations. As long as you know a procedure you can figure out an answer.	Simplify the expression: $(2 \times 4) + 14 \div 7$
Visual Spatial Reasoning • Involves the ability to see relationships that are displayed graphically. May require conceptual and/or contextual understanding.	How many squares do you see?
Use of Tools • Requires the understanding of the function of a tool, how and when to use that tool flexibly, appropriately and strategically.	
Vocabulary/Use of Terms • Requires the understanding of mathematical terms in order to make sense of the question or mathematics ideas.	Which of the following is **not** a property of a trapezoid? a) is convex polygon b) has 360 degrees c) has a pair of parallel lines d) is a quadrangle
Symbols • Requires the understanding of mathematical symbols in order to make sense of the question, mathematics ideas, and/or solutions.	$\|4\|$ π % $\leq$ $\sqrt{}$ /

Test-Savvy Math By Christine King, © 2013 CKingEducation, Inc.

NAME: _____   DATE: _____

Sample QUESTION CATEGORY

Question	Category	Reason
Which equations would be true if you put 24 on the blank like? 1) ____ = 10 + 10 + 4 2) 16 + 24 = ____ + 16 3) 34 − ____ = 34 − 14 − 10 A) Equation 1 B) Equations 1 and 2 C) Equations 2 and 3 D) Equations 1, 2, and 3 Grade 3 – Multiple-Choice	☑ Concepts ☐ Procedure ☐ Visual/Spatial Reasoning ☐ Use of Tools ☐ Vocabulary ☐ Symbols	This is a conceptual question, because you do not have to do any calculations. If you understand the Commutative Property of Addition and how to decompose numbers by place value, then choice D becomes evident.
Jamie wanted to draw an obtuse angle. Shown below is what he drew. Did Jamie draw an obtuse angle? Explain your answer. 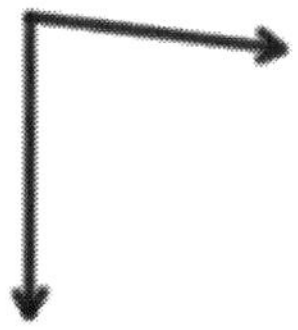 What is the measure of the angle drawn? Grade 4 – Extended Response	☐ Concepts ☐ Procedure ☑ Visual/Spatial Reasoning ☑ Use of Tools ☑ Vocabulary ☐ Symbols	We need to use our visual/spatial reasoning skills when trying to "see" the angle. We need to know how to use a protector to figure out the measurement of the angle. We need to understand the vocabulary of "obtuse angle" to explain our thinking.
Create a word problem for the expression below, and then solve your word problem. $$(10 \cdot 4 + 5)/3^2$$ Grade 5 – Extended Response	☑ Concepts ☑ Procedure ☐ Visual/Spatial Reasoning ☐ Use of Tools ☐ Vocabulary ☑ Symbols	We need to understand the concepts of addition, multiplication, and exponentiation in order to write a realistic word problem. We can follow the procedure for the Order of Operations to evaluate the expression. We need to understand what the symbols mean in the equation in order to evaluate it correctly.

Today was the Big Day

"Our students tested today. They were as most kids are on standardized days...they were focused. Of course they said the test was easy."

— CMK, May, 2011

I started writing this post almost a year ago, but was never inspired to finish it. I am not really inspired right now either. What I am is another adjective...frustrated. Most of my schools are focused on...guess what...testing. They say, "We have six-weeks, how do I best prep my students?"

Everyone is looking for a magic pill to give students, so that they know and understand all of the content that we are spoon feeding them. It won't work. I have hope that with the coming of the Common Core State Standards educators are prompted to take another look at how we prepare students for standardized testing.

More test-prep is not the answer. Test-savviness is an alternative. We have to build thinking and reasoning into the test-prep process and it needs to be grounded in research-based instructional practices that raise the cognitive demand levels of students.

Excerpt from post at "Test-Savvy Math" at http://testsavvymath.blogspot.com

#6 I REVIEW

LEARNING OBJECTIVE
Students will be able to identify, discuss, analyze, and explain common errors and trends on exam items.

GUIDING QUESTIONS
• Why do you think that question gave students trouble?
• What strategies can you suggest to help others students with this type of exam question?

MATERIALS
• Template: I Review
• Item analysis from exam
• Reference resources

TEST-SAVVY SKILLS
• Generates their own problems & solutions
• Discusses/critiques solutions
• Identifies common misconceptions related to concepts
• Identifies/categorizes question types
• Develops visual memory of the exam format
• Is self-reflective, critical of work
• Seeks out, identifies, explains, and replicates errors as tools for learning
• Analyzes data and identifies personal trends
• Perseveres, is flexible even when questions are challenging, and has alternative strategies

MATHEMATICAL PRACTICES	
1	Make sense of problems and persevere in solving them
3	Construct viable arguments and critique the reasoning of others
4	Model with mathematics
5	Use appropriate tools strategically
6	Attend to precision

ACTIVITY SUMMARY

Students work collaboratively to review and teach the class items from an exam that was previously given and graded. This strategy can be used with all exam types (i.e. multiple-choice, constructed response, fill in the blank, etc.), but is described for use with constructed response questions.

TIME: 45 minutes when introducing the activity, 20 minutes when revisited

SET UP

1. Grade student papers and create an item analysis for each question.
2. Place students into groups of 3 – 4 based upon the data.
3. Assign 1 – 3 questions per group based upon the identified needs and data from the exam being reviewed.

ACTIVITY IN ACTION

1. Teacher provides each group with an item analysis sheet from the exam for the groups to analyze.
2. Teacher tells each group the questions that they are going to analyze.
3. Students analyze their questions by completing the "I Review Template".
4. Students work collaboratively to verify and justify their answer(s).
5. A student from the group goes to the other groups and finds out what other students in the class might have answered for that problem.
6. The group analyzes the mistakes that others students made and provides strategies to help others not make those same errors again.
7. Groups review/teach their problems with the class.

ASSESSMENT

- Can the students correctly solve the problem?
- Can the students identify any additional methods/strategies to solve the problems?

EXTENSIONS

- 5-Minute I Review Videos: Each day students review a problem for the class. Record the review/teach and make it available for students to access at a later time.
- Strategy Wall/Book: Have students put together a wall or a book of strategies to help students solve or check specific question types.

FAQ

Q: How do I create an item-analysis?
A: If you are not using an automated scanning system that will generate an item analysis, then you simply have to simply have to calculate the amount correct per question. Some teachers create a grid where they can check-off correct responses by question and student. Some teachers have a grid for each question, so that they can also note incorrect responses. (See the next page for examples.)

Q: How does the activity change if my test only has multiple-choice questions?
A: You would eliminate Step #5 as a student would not need to collect incorrect responses, because they would be listed on the student exam papers.

GROUP MEMBERS: _____   DATE: _____

Sample 1 REVIEW ITEM ANALYSIS

Exam: District Benchmark #1	Date Given: Oct. 15	Grade Level: 5
Item #: 23	% Correct: 30%	% Incorrect: 70%

Misconception in Distractor Selected:
(What was the test-maker trap that most of the students fell into?)

The problem asked, "How many days would 2880 minutes be?" This was a multi-step problem, but most of the students only did one step. For the students that chose 120, they did: 2880 ÷ 24. We think they meant 24 to be 24 hours in a day. But what the 24 was showing was that we made 24 groups with 120 minutes in each or 2 hours per group. To find the number of days in 2880 minutes days we would have to divide the 2880 minutes by 60 minutes to find out how groups of 60 minutes (1 hour) that we have.

Suggested Strategy to Avoid Trap:

- Write out the conversion in words.
- Make a table or a diagram when dealing with conversions of units.

24 groups × 60 minutes = 1 day in minutes = 1440 minutes

Day	Minutes
1	1440
2	2880

2880 minutes divided by 60 minutes will tell how many groups of 60 minutes we can make or how many groups of 1 hour we can make. 2880/60 = 48 hours or 2 days

Exam: District Benchmark #1	Date Given: Oct. 15	Grade Level: 5
Item #: 15	% Correct: 45%	% Incorrect: 55%

Misconception in Distractor Selected:
(What was the test-maker trap that most of the students fell into?)

The problem asked us figure out how 1/3 and 3/6 of 24 gum drops were combined. About 15% students added 1/3 and 3/6 incorrectly and selected 4/9. They did not realize that you cannot add unlike units and have to convert the fractions to like units. The rest of the students who had the problem incorrect added correctly getting 5/6, but did not find out how much 5/6 was of 24.

Suggested Strategy to Avoid Trap:

- Make a math sketch to see the problem better.
- Use a bar diagram to help figure out the problem.

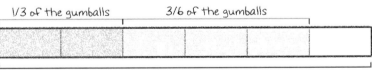

24 gumballs divided into 6 groups = 4 gumballs per group
5 groups with 4 gumballs in each = 20 gumballs
5/6 of 24 is 20 or 5/6 × 24 = 20

Test-Savvy Math By Christine King, © 2013 CKingEducation, Inc.

#7 TWO ARGUMENTS

LEARNING OBJECTIVE
Students will be able to make a mathematical argument about a situation and use various tools/strategies as proof.
GUIDING QUESTIONS
• How can your convince us that your reasoning is mathematically true?
MATERIALS
• Template: Two Arguments
• 2 opposing points of view/reasoning on a single item
TEST-SAVVY SKILLS
• Manipulates mathematical ideas as applied to real-world contexts
• Discusses/critiques solutions
• Identifies common misconceptions related to concepts
• Seeks out, identifies, explains, and replicates errors as tools for learning
• Perseveres, is flexible even when questions are challenging, and has alternative strategies

	MATHEATICAL PRACTICES
1	Make sense of problems and persevere in solving them
2	Reason abstractly and quantitatively
3	Construct viable arguments and critique the reasoning of others
4	Model with mathematics
5	Use appropriate tools strategically
6	Attend to precision
7	Look for and make use of structure
8	Look for and express repeated regularity in reasoning

ACTIVITY SUMMARY
Students are presented with two different mathematical arguments and they have to convince the class which argument is mathematically true by justifying one of the positions. (*Lesson idea adapted from "Two Arguments Energizer" by Dr. Nicki Newton.*)

TIME: 15 minutes when introducing the activity, 5 – 10 minutes when revisited

SET UP
1. Determine the two arguments to be used based upon formative assessment conversations that you have had with your students.
2. Have the resources or tools needed to help your students prove their arguments.

ACTIVITY IN ACTION
1. Students are presented with the two arguments and asked to read each one, and then side with one of the arguments.
2. Students discuss their position with a partner or small-group.
3. Students complete the "Two Arguments" sheet.
4. The teacher selects students to justify each argument. The debate ends when the whole class is convinced of one side. Students write about why one argument is mathematically true and the other is not. Student can also reflect on how their thinking has changed during the course of the discussion.

ASSESSMENT
- Can the students make valid mathematical arguments?
- Can the students come up with multiple strategies or ways of explaining or showing their thinking?

EXTENSIONS
- Math Debate: Have a mathematical debate where students can work on teams and classmates can select who had the most accurate, precise, and valid arguments.
- Have students create their own "Two Arguments" based upon the misconceptions that they note on a particular topic.

FAQ
Q: What if the class does not ever come to consensus?
A: That is possible especially when students have a very fragile understanding of a concept or if the arguments are too similar. It is not essential that the class comes to consensus, but it is essential that you understand why students are unable to come to consensus. It is also vital that you understand who was not able to see or understand the argument that was mathematically true. This group might require re-teaching in a small-group.

Q: Can we use arguments that are both valid, but different?
A: Yes. This is a great way to help other students become flexible in seeing the argument of others. You might have to wrap up the discussion or guide the students if they do not realize that both arguments are valid.

NAME: _____   DATE: _____

Sample TWO ARGUMENTS

Scenario

(Problem adapted from Illustrative Mathematics – Alignment: 4.NF.A)

Erica and Cruz were both getting ready for soccer. Erica ran 2 laps around the playground. Cruz ran 1 lap around the school.

Argument #1	Argument #2
Erica said, "I ran more laps, so I ran farther."	Cruz said, "Four laps around the school is 1 mile, but it takes 12 laps around the playground to go 1 mile. My laps are much longer, so I ran farther."

Decide and Defend

Whom do you agree with?

I agree with Cruz.

Why? *(Use Numbers, Words and a Model to defend your thinking.)*

I agreed with…because…

I agree with Cruz, because his laps are much longer. To prove my point I made a math sketch. The one lap that Cruz ran is $\frac{1}{4}$ of a mile. The 2 laps that Erica ran is $\frac{2}{12}$ of a mile. One $\frac{1}{4}$ of a mile is more than $\frac{2}{12}$ of a mile, so Cruz ran farther.

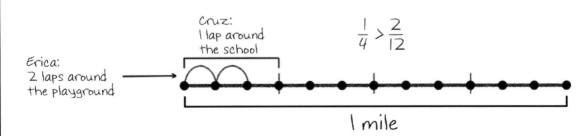

4 laps around the school is 1 mile = 12 laps around the playground is 1 mile

Test-Savvy Math By Christine King, © 2013 CKingEducation, Inc.

#8 COLLABORATIVE EXPLANATION

LEARNING OBJECTIVE
Students will be able to write a complete and well thought out explanation to a problem.

GUIDING QUESTIONS
- Does your final explanation make sense?
- Was this more challenging than writing an explanation on your own?

MATERIALS
- Colored pens/pencils
- Template: Collaborative Written Explanation
- Problem students have solved previously

TEST-SAVVY SKILLS
- Manipulates mathematical ideas as applied to real-world contexts
- Generates their own problems & solutions
- Discusses/critiques solutions
- Understands how math terms are related and relate terms to other math concepts
- Develops visual memory of the exam format
- Is self-reflective, critical of work
- Perseveres, is flexible even when questions are challenging, and has alternative strategies

MATHEMATICAL PRACTICES
1. Make sense of problems and persevere in solving them
2. Reason abstractly and quantitatively
3. Construct viable arguments and critique the reasoning of others
6. Attend to precision
7. Look for and make use of structure
8. Look for and express repeated regularity in reasoning

ACTIVITY SUMMARY
Students collaboratively write a written explanation for a problem that they have solved independently or previously.

TIME: 20 minutes when introducing the activity, 10 – 15 minutes when revisited

SETUP:
1. Select a problem that students have worked out previously. You may choose to differentiate by focusing certain groups of students on specific topics. If so, then select different problems for each group of students. Groups should have between 3 to 4 students.
2. Have different colored pens or colored pencils available for students to use. You may wish to have a chart to show which students are to use which colored pen/pencil.

ACTIVITY IN ACTION
1. Explain the activity to the students.
2. Give students a chance to review the problem and discuss the problem within their groups.
3. The activity begins with each student writing the first sentence of the written explanation for the problem. Students should be given about 1 minute for this part.
4. The activity continues by rotating the papers in a clockwise or counter-clockwise fashion. Give students additional time for each new rotation. For example, you might give students 1 ½ minutes for the second rotation, but 2 minutes for the third rotation.
5. After all the rotations are completed, papers are returned to the original student for review.
6. The group can discuss how to craft an even better explanation, by selecting the best lines from all the papers.

ASSESSMENT
- Do the students know how to begin a written explanation?
- Can the students interpret/make sense of what a classmate in saying?
- Can the students create a model written explanation?

EXTENSIONS
- Math Centers: Use during small-group instruction, but this time give students the first line or give students the last line.
- Make a book of mathematical explanations to problems, showing the before and after to model student growth.

FAQ
Q: I tried this with my students. It worked for the most part, but some students were stuck, because the papers that they received just did not make sense to them and they did not know how to continue. What should I do?

A: This may happen the first few times when implementing the activity. Highlight sentences might cause students to become stuck and model how we could move beyond that point.

STUDENT 1: _____ STUDENT 2: _____

STUDENT 3: _____ STUDENT 4: _____

Sample COLLABORATIVE EXPLANATION

Original Problem
(Problem from Illustrative Mathematics – Alignment: 4.MD.A.3, 4.OA.A.3)

Karl's rectangular vegetable garden is 20 feet by 45 feet, and Makenna's is 25 feet by 40 feet. Whose garden is larger in area?

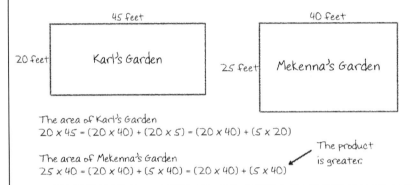

The area of Karl's Garden
20 × 45 = (20 × 40) + (20 × 5) = (20 × 40) + (5 × 20)

The area of Mekenna's Garden
25 × 40 = (20 × 40) + (5 × 40) = (20 × 40) + (5 × 40) ← The product is greater.

Explanation*

Mekenna's garden is larger is area. To solve the problem I first drew rectangles to show Karl's garden and Mekenna's garden. **Next, I used the Distributive Property of Multiplication over Addition and the Commutative Property of Multiplication to prove that Mekenna's garden was larger in area.** *I was able to show that both gardens have an equivalent area of 20 × 40 or 800 square feet, but Mekenna's garden also had 5 × 40 or 200 square feet more, while Karl's garden only had an additional 5 × 20 or 100 square feet more.*

*Please note: Each font variation represents a different students' contribution to the Collaborative Explanation.

Section 2

TAPPING INTO PRIOR KNOWLEDGE

How do we know what we know? As human beings, we automate or habitualize much of what we do and how we think based upon what we know. *Test-Savvy Math: Fostering Thinking and Reasoning into the Test-Prep Process* supports the idea that, in order "to increase or extend our knowledge" we must challenge, question, and examine what we know as a mechanism for providing the foundational support our mind needs to incorporate new learning.

The activities detailed in Section 2 provide opportunities for students to explore, document, and connect prior knowledge to their current understandings. With consistent use, these strategies can help students to develop mental routines that automatically seek out related knowledge and understandings.

PONDER THIS...

- Prior knowledge fundamentally influences all learning (Altman, 2002).

- Prior knowledge is personal, complex and highly resistant to change (Jensen, 2005, p. 45).

- Students do not passively absorb information; they approach a new situation with prior knowledge. As they assimilate new information, they form their own meanings (Moon & Schulman, 1995, p.5).

- The most important single factor influencing learning is what the learner already knows (Ausubel's Learning Theory).

- A particularly important type of metacognitive thinking in mathematics is coordinating conclusions drawn from alternative mathematical representations or strategies. In other words, we want to encourage students to think about problems not only in multiple ways (strategies), but also with multiple tools (representations), and to draw conclusions that are not only quantitative (numeric answers), but also qualitative (verbal interpretations) Excerpt from *How Students Learn Mathematics in the Classroom*, 2005, p.372.

LEARNING OBJECTIVE
Students will be able to associate math concepts and connect then to a real-life context.

GUIDING QUESTIONS
• Why does that word fit with the others?
• What math concepts do these words connect to? Why?
• What other math terms could you have used and still convey the same meaning?

MATERIALS
• Template: Concept Square
• Reference materials (optional)

TEST-SAVVY SKILLS
• Manipulates mathematical ideas as applied to real-world contexts
• Discusses/critiques solutions
• Understands how math terms are related and relate terms to other math concepts
• Is self-reflective, critical of work

MATHEMATICAL PRACTICES	
1	Make sense of problems and persevere in solving them
3	Construct viable arguments and critique the reasoning of others
6	Attend to precision
8	Look for and express repeated regularity in reasoning

#9 CONCEPT SQUARE

ACTIVITY SUMMARY
Students work collaboratively to complete a "Concept Square" by tapping into their prior knowledge and associating mathematical terms related to a specific topic.

TIME: 45 minutes when introducing the activity, 15 – 30 minutes when revisited

ACTIVITY IN ACTION
1. The teacher distributes the Concept Square Template to students and gives the class or each group a topic/area of focus, (i.e. fractions, circumference, algebra, etc.)
2. The first student writes down a term related to the topic.
3. The next student writes down a related term in the next available box.
4. The 3rd and 4th students repeat step #3.
5. The students discuss the terms and determine if all the terms "fit" into the Word Square.
6. Once the students are in agreement as to all the terms that "fit" into the Word Square, they write a 3 to 4 sentence paragraph using all the terms.

ASSESSMENT
- Are the terms used related?
- Does the paragraph make mathematical sense?
- What is revealed by the terms chosen?

EXTENSIONS
- **Create a Question:** Students create exam questions where the terms or the concepts are embodied in the question.
- **Math Essay:** If several groups or the whole class focused on a single topic they could review their paragraphs and develop a mathematical essay on the topic.
- **First Draft:** Use the paragraph produced as a first draft allowing students to edit and improve on what was written.

FAQ
Q: This task does not involve math per se, is that ok?

A: The task may not involve mathematical computations, but it does involve math. Math is a process of articulating and defining our world. Math is a process of applying meaning and order to life and communication via mathematics. Words are the vehicle through which we achieve that end. Standardized exams require students to process and comprehend large amounts of mathematical vocabulary (Tileston, 2004) and this activity is a collaborative way to provide students with the opportunity.

NAME: DATE:

Sample CONCEPT SQUARE

Topic: Measurement

unit	inches	Yards and inches are units in the Customary Measurement System. **We use the Customary System in America.** Other parts of the world and scientists use the Metric System. The Metric System has units like centimeters, which are very small.
Centimeters	yards	

Topic: Functions

relationships	graphs	A function shows mathematical relationships, when one thing affects another. **We are learning about linear functions.** We can show linear functions on a graph. You can use a ratio table, which is another name for an input/output table, to help figure out if there is a functional relationship.
Ratio table	linear functions	

*Please note: Each font variation represents a different students' contribution to the Collaborative Explanation.

#10 FRAYER MODEL PROBLEM SOLVING

LEARNING OBJECTIVE
Students will be able to identify and explain the mathematically relevant facts in a word problem.

GUIDING QUESTIONS
• How did you select which information was important?
• How can you convince me that this information is not important?

MATERIALS
• Template: Frayer Model Problem Solving
• word problem

TEST-SAVVY SKILLS
• Manipulates mathematical ideas as applied to real-world contexts
• Generates their own problems & solutions
• Discusses/critiques solutions
• Understands how math terms are related and relate terms to other math concepts
• Develops visual memory of the exam format
• Perseveres, is flexible even when questions are challenging, and has alternative strategies

MATHEATICAL PRACTICES	
1	Make sense of problems and persevere in solving them
2	Reason abstractly and quantitatively
3	Construct viable arguments and critique the reasoning of others
4	Model with mathematics
5	Use appropriate tools strategically
6	Attend to precision
7	Look for and make use of structure
8	Look for and express repeated regularity in reasoning

ACTIVITY SUMMARY

Students analyze a word problem by looking at the facts presented, why the facts are important, and why some information is not important.

TIME: 30 minutes when introducing the activity, 10 – 15 minutes when revisited

ACTIVITY IN ACTION

1. Explain to the students what they are going to do in each section.
2. Students read the problem, and then discuss what to write in the "Facts" section.
3. Before they move on to another section, they give their paper to another group to review and give feedback on.
4. Once the original group gets the paper back, they review the feedback and update the reviewed section as needed.
5. The group then goes on to complete the "Why Important?" and "Why Not Important?" sections.
6. They repeat steps #3 and #4 and then complete the "Operations Involved" section.
7. Class discusses how they knew that certain things were facts and how this can help them when looking at other word problems.

ASSESSMENT

- Can the students determine which facts are important to the problem?
- How do the students justify what is important when solving the problem?

EXTENSIONS

- Pre-Assembled Facts: Give the students two facts and have them determine why these facts are important.
- Irrelevant Fact: Give the students a list of facts, but place 1 fact in the list that does not belong.
- What is the Problem?: Give the facts, the why and why not information and ask the students to come up with the problem.

FAQ

Q: It seems like a lot to write. How can I adapt this activity?
A: You could have the students verbalize instead of writing in each section. You could serve as the scribe. You could use a recorder. You could do the activity with the whole class and have a group record information for 1 section. Each day you could record information in just one section, until each section is complete.

NAME: _____   DATE: _____

Sample FRAYER MODEL PROBLEM SOLVING

Problem

On Fridays Matt and Pam go to McDonald's. Matt gets 3 hamburgers and Pam gets 1 hamburger. Each hamburger costs $2. How much money would they spend on hamburgers in 4 weeks?

Important Math Facts

- 3 hamburgers
- 1 hamburger
- $2 per hamburger
- 4 weeks
- 4 Fridays

Operation(s) Involved

Adding the hamburgers (3 + 1)

Multiplying the total hamburgers by $2

Multiplying the total cost of the hamburgers by 4 for the 4 Fridays

Why Important?

- We have to know about how many hamburgers, because that will help us figure out how many they bought.
- If we figure out how many hamburgers they bought, then we know that they spent $2 for every hamburger.
- We know that they bought 3+1 hamburgers or 4 hamburgers every Friday for 4 weeks. They did this for 4 Fridays, since each week has a Friday.

Why Not Important?

- The names of the people are not important, because that will not help us figure out how much money they spend in 4 weeks.
- The name of the restaurant is not important, because it does not help us figure out how much they spent.
- The day of the week is not important. We just needed to know that they went 1 time every week.

Teacher Notes/Peer Comments

Test-Savvy Math By Christine King, © 2013 CKingEducation, Inc.

#11 RALLY ROUND THE PROBLEM

LEARNING OBJECTIVE
Students will be able to identify and associate math concepts given the situation presented in a word problem.
GUIDING QUESTIONS
• What big math concept(s) do you think you would learn more about or be practicing by doing this problem? • What words would you eliminate off of your list? Why?
MATERIALS
• Template: Rally Round the Problem • a word problem • Math Word Wall or reference materials
TEST-SAVVY SKILLS
• Manipulates mathematical ideas as applied to real-world contexts • Generates their own problems & solutions • Discusses/critiques solutions • Identifies/categorizes question types • Understands how math terms are related and relate terms to other math concepts • Perseveres, is flexible even when questions are challenging, and has alternative strategies
MATHEATICAL PRACTICES
1 Make sense of problems and persevere in solving them 3 Construct viable arguments and critique the reasoning of others 6 Attend to precision 7 Look for and make use of structure 8 Look for and express repeated regularity in reasoning

ACTIVITY SUMMARY
Students will examine a word problem by looking at the math terms that are associated with the problem.

TIME: 45 minutes when introducing the activity, 15 – 30 minutes when revisited

SET-UP
1. Select 4 to 6 problems for the class.
2. Place each problem on different colored paper.
3. Arrange students into pairs.
4. Determine the problems that each group will get.

ACTIVITY IN ACTION
1. Explain to the students that they will be working with others on a problem.
2. Model the steps of "Rally Round the Problem."
3. Distribute problems.
4. Students follow the steps of "Rally Round the Problem."

ASSESSMENT
- Are the math vocabulary terms that the students listed related to the problem or are they just random math words?
- Can the students justify and argue their mathematical thinking and solutions?

EXTENSIONS
- Make a "Rally Round the Problem" game by displaying a math word problem and having the students play in teams to generate math terms. In order to keep the terms generated, the teams have to justify the math terms listed and convince the other team that they belong in the list.
- Explain the mathematics in the problem or how the problem was solved by incorporating the relevant words from the list of words generated.

FAQ
Q: If I am only using 4 to 6 problem, how does every pair get a problem when I have a class of 28 students?
A: In order to complete the last step of "Rally Round the Problem" students need to get together with other students who had the same problem as they did. This process of "revisiting" allows students to delve into the problem more deeply. They see the words that other groups came up with and have the chance to discuss and justify how they resolved the problem. During the "revisiting" phase students can add to or edit their work. So, while you may only use 4 to 6 problems, all pairs will have a problem.

Q: Can I have my students share out what they learned during the "revisiting" phase?
A: Yes. Once students have discussed, added to and/or edited their work during the "revisiting" phase, having a whole group that may have had the question on averaging share out is an excellent idea.

NAME: _____ DATE: _____

Sample RALLY ROUND THE PROBLEM

1. **READ** the problem and identify the math terms used in the problem.
2. **RALLY** Round the Problem by writing other terms that can be associated with that problem.
3. **REFLECT** on the terms generated and highlight or circle the one that you think will help you solve the problem.
4. **RESOLVE** the problem.
5. **REVISIT** the solution by teaming up with other students who have similar problems and discuss your solutions.

THE PROBLEM
(Problem from Illustrative Mathematics, Alignment 6: RP.A.3, 6.G.A)

Alexis needs to paint the four exterior walls of a large rectangular barn. The length of the barn is 80 feet, the width is 50 feet, and the height is 30 feet. The paint costs $28 per gallon, and each gallon covers 420 square feet. How much will it cost Alexis to paint the barn? Explain your work.

MATH TERMS	WORK OUT THE PROBLEM
rectangular (length) feet width gallon square feet volume (area) adding multiplying money	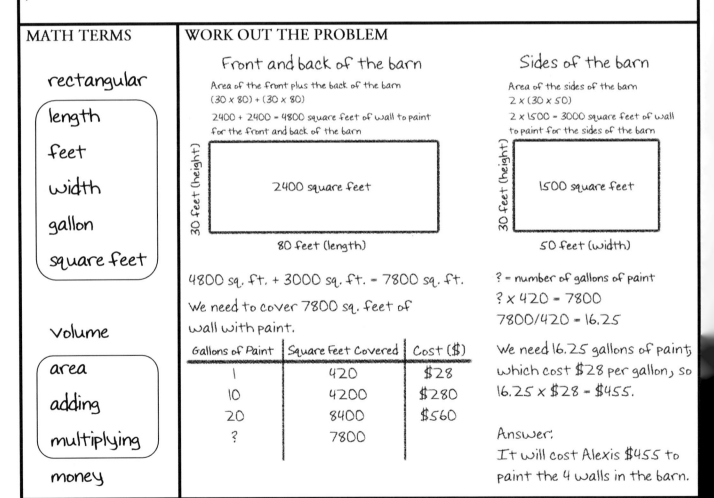

TEACHER COMMENTS

Section 3

REPRESENTING MATH

Mathematical Practice #4: Model with Mathematics calls for students to be flexible in representing real-world situations using mathematics beyond the use of abstract equations in isolation. Students are expected to consistently show their understanding using mathematical sketches, diagrams, number lines, tables or other math models.

The activities detailed in Section 3 provide opportunities for students to visualize and interpret how they and others "see" the mathematics embedded within a problem solving situation. With consistent use, these strategies can help students to develop and refine ways to quickly understand numerical relationships and what problems are saying and asking.

PONDER THIS...

- Drawing diagrams to represent a problem does facilitate a student's search for a "relevant" solution for the problem (Larkin and Simon, 1987).

- Students who have difficulty representing math problems will have difficulty solving them. Effective visual representations, whether on paper or in one's imagination, show the relationships among problem parts (Montague, 2004).

- So What Should We See in an Effective Mathematics Classroom?
    - Frequent use of pictorial representations to help students visualize the mathematics they are learning.
    - Frequent use of the number line and bar models to represent numbers and word problems.
    - Frequent opportunities for students to draw or show and then describe what is drawn or shown (Excerpt from *Accessible Mathematics: 10 Instructional Shifts That Raise Student Achievement* by Steven Leinwand, 2009).

#12 MATCH THE MATH PICTURE

LEARNING OBJECTIVE
Students will be able to represent and explain how they are visualizing word problems given the situation.
GUIDING QUESTIONS
• Can you explain how you see the situation?
• Can you show me how you represented all of the mathematically relevant information in this situation?
• Why do you think this representation matches that word problem?
MATERIALS
• word problems that are easy to visualize
• scrap paper to sketch
TEST-SAVVY SKILLS
• Manipulates mathematical ideas as applied to real-world contexts
• Generates their own problems & solutions
• Discusses/critiques solutions
• Is self-reflective, critical of work
• Perseveres, is flexible even when questions are challenging, and has alternative strategies

MATHEMATICAL PRACTICES	
1	Make sense of problems and persevere in solving them
2	Reason abstractly and quantitatively
3	Construct viable arguments and critique the reasoning of others
4	Model with mathematics
6	Attend to precision
7	Look for and make use of structure
8	Look for and express repeated regularity in reasoning

ACTIVITY SUMMARY
Students will work on visualizing math word problems by creating and matching mathematical sketches with word problem situations.

TIME: 45 minutes when introducing the activity, 10 – 15 minutes when revisited

SET-UP
1. Put together sets of 2 to 3 problems for each pair/group of students. Use different colored paper for each set of problems.
2. Cut up scrap paper into workable sizes of 3 x 4 inch portions. Use scrap paper that is the same color as the paper used for the problem set. This will help keep track of the problem sets and the mathematical sketches that should match them.

ACTIVITY IN ACTION
1. Students work in pairs or small-groups to create mathematical sketches for a set of problems that they were given. Every pair or small-group should have a different set of questions.
2. Once the students have completed their mathematical sketches for their problem sets, then problems and newly created mathematical sketches are exchanged with other pairs/groups.
3. Students work collaboratively to analyze and match the mathematical sketches with the problems.
4. Once they have matched all of the problems and mathematical sketches, they write (or tell) suggestions for improving upon the mathematical sketches drawn.

ASSESSMENT
- Can the student make a mathematical sketch for the problems given?
- Is the mathematical sketch precise and labeled appropriately given the context of the word problem?
- Does the mathematical sketch make sense given the context?

EXTENSIONS
- Make a Book of Mathematical Sketches: This can be a great study tool, resource and a way for teachers and students to track progress over time.
- Translated into Math Models: Have students change a mathematical sketch into a table/chart, a number line or a bar diagram to convey the same information from the original problem.
- Use a similar idea, but now match the mathematical sketch to an expression or equation.

FAQ
Q: Does each pair or small-group have to have a different set of problems?
A: No. Depending on the size of your class, you can have two or three sets of students working on creating mathematical sketches for the same set of problems, but they would still work with one partner or in their small-group. After they have finished making their mathematical sketches, then they would compare their work with the others in the classroom that had similar problem sets.

NAME: _____   DATE: _____

Sample MATCH THE MATHEMATICAL PICTURE

MATH PROBLEM	MATHEMATICAL SKETCH
Sophie made 52 cupcakes for the school bake sale. Each cupcake costs $0.50. If she made $10, how many cupcakes does she still have left to sell?	Key: ◯ = 2 cupcakes Cupcakes made by Sophie 52 cupcakes ◯◯◯◯◯◯◯◯◯◯◯◯◯ ◯◯◯◯◯◯◯◯◯◯◯◯◯ Cupcakes made by Elizabeth 26 cupcakes ◯◯◯◯◯◯◯◯◯◯◯◯◯
Sophie made 52 cupcakes for the school bake sale. She packed them a dozen at a time into boxes to take to school. How may boxes will she need?	Key: ◯ = 2 cupcakes [◯ ◯ ◯ ◯ ◯ $1.00 $1.00 $1.00 $1.00 $1.00 ◯ ◯ ◯ ◯ ◯ $1.00 $1.00 $1.00 $1.00 $1.00] cupcakes that were sold ◯ ◯ ◯ ◯ ◯ ◯ ◯ ◯ ◯ ◯ cupcakes that were not sold ◯ ◯ ◯ ◯ ◯ ◯
Sophie made 52 cupcakes for the school bake sale. Her best friend, Elizabeth, made half as many cupcakes. How many cupcakes did the girls make for the school bake sale?	Key: ◯ = 2 cupcakes 1st Box: [◯ ◯ ◯ ◯ ◯ ◯] 2nd Box: [◯ ◯ ◯ ◯ ◯ ◯] 3rd Box: [◯ ◯ ◯ ◯ ◯ ◯] 4th Box: [◯ ◯ ◯ ◯ ◯ ◯] 5th Box: [◯ ◯]

Test-Savvy Math By Christine King, © 2013 CKingEducation, Inc.

#13 SHOW ME IN MANY WAYS

LEARNING OBJECTIVE
Students will be able to model with mathematics using a variety of strategies and representations.
GUIDING QUESTIONS
• How does their way compare to your way? • Which way is more mathematically precise given the context? How do you know? • Why does that way make sense to you?
MATERIALS
• a constructed response question • Show Me in Many Ways Template
TEST-SAVVY SKILLS
• Generates their own problems & solutions • Discusses/critiques solutions • Identifies common misconceptions related to concepts • Is self-reflective, critical of work • Perseveres, is flexible even when questions are challenging, and has alternative strategies
MATHEATICAL PRACTICES
1 Make sense of problems and persevere in solving them
2 Reason abstractly and quantitatively
3 Construct viable arguments and critique the reasoning of others
4 Model with mathematics
5 Use appropriate tools strategically
6 Attend to precision
7 Look for and make use of structure
8 Look for and express repeated regularity in reasoning

ACTIVITY SUMMARY
Students collaborate to find various ways to show solutions to constructed response questions. Solution pathways could include alternative algorithms, tables/charts, diagrams, number lines or other pictorial representations.

TIME: 45 minutes when introducing the activity, 30 minutes when revisited

ACTIVITY IN ACTION
1. Students solve the problem as "Do Now" or for HW.
2. The teacher reviews the student work, noting different strategies.
3. Teacher selects 3 students to share and explain their strategies.
4. Students copy and discuss the alternative strategies and student misconceptions about the math involved and the strategies/algorithms used.

ASSESSMENT
• Can the students explain an alternative strategy?
• Can the students compare and contrast an alternative to their own?

EXTENSIONS
• **Apply the Strategy:** Either as a whole class or in small groups, students can work to apply alternative strategies in similar problems.
• **Representational to Abstract:** In small groups discuss the connection of charts, diagrams or pictorial representations to abstract representations. For example, how does the pictorial representation ••• ••• relate to 2 x 3?
• **Make a Poster:** Have students work together to make a poster that shows multiple ways to solve a problem. This poster can be used as a reference for students and/or a study guide.

FAQ
Q: Do I always have to use constructed response questions?
A: No, any type of question will work. However, students generally have to show their work on constructed response questions, so you want them to have multiple solution options at their disposal.

Q: What if my students all come up with the same strategy?
A: This is a common issue, especially if students are accustomed to only showing solutions in one way. As the teacher you might have to have alternative solutions charted and ready to show and discuss with your students. I usually give the strategy a student name and a mathematical name, i.e. Jamie's Way (The Associative Property of Multiplication).

Q: How often should I use this strategy?
A: Formally, you might only use this strategy a few times during a unit of study. Informally, you may incorporate the ideas behind this strategy on a daily basis by encouraging students to share their various solutions. When planning a unit of study you may explicitly outline and chart various strategies that you want to promote. During the unit students could then refer back to your charts and select strategies to utilize.

NAME: _____   DATE: _____

Sample SHOW ME IN MANY WAYS

Problem:
(Adapted from Illustrative Mathematics, "Selling Computers" Alignment 1: 7.RP.A.3)

The sales division King's Car Dealership sold 24 cars last month. Their competitor, Crush Cars, sold 25% more cars than they did for the same time period. If King's Car Dealership wants to sell at least 10% more cars this month than what the Crush Cars dealership sold last month, how many cars would have to sell?

Tony's Way

King's Car Dealership: 24 cars = 100%

Crush Cars: x = 125%

Calculations:
24 × 125 = 100x
3000 = 100x
3000/100 = x
30 = x = the # of cars sold last month at Crush Cars

10% of 30 is 3
30 + 3 = 33
King's Car Dealership would have to sell 33 or more cars this month to sell at least 10% more cars than Crush Cars did last month.

Lani's Way

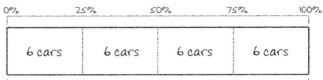

24 Cars sold at King's Car Dealership last month

24/4 = 6

25% of 24 cars is 6 cars, so Crush Cars sold 6 more cars last month than King's Dealership.
24 + 6 = 30 cars

10% or one-tenth of 30 is 3

King's Car Dealership has to sell 33 cars or more to beat Crush Cars this month. So they have to sell about 10 more cars than they did last month.

Xavier's Way

Number of Cars Sold	24	36	30
Percent Increase	0%	50%	25%

↑ # of cars sold last month by King's Cars

↑ # of cars sold last month by Crush Cars with the 25% increase compared to King's Cars

30 cars split into 10 equal groups gives me 3 cars per group, which is another way to say 10% of 30 is 3.

30 cars + 3 cars = 33 cars

They have to sell at least 33 cars.

Tina's Way

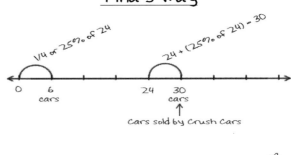

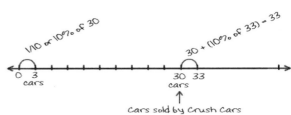

To sell 10% more than what Crush Cars sold, King's Car Dealership would need to sell 34 cars or more.

#14 VERBAL VISUAL WORD ASSOCIATION (VVWA)

LEARNING OBJECTIVE
Students will be able to make real-life and pictorial connections when seeing or hearing math terms.
GUIDING QUESTIONS
• How is your representation of the math term similar or different from his/hers? • After looking at the work of other students, how would you improve or change your representations?
MATERIALS
• a multiple-choice problem • Word Problem Rework Template
TEST-SAVVY SKILLS
• Manipulates mathematical ideas as applied to real-world contexts • Generates their own problems & solutions • Discusses/critiques solutions • Identifies common misconceptions related to concepts • Understands how math terms are related and relate terms to other math concepts • Is self-reflective, critical of work • Analyzes data and identifies personal trends • Perseveres, is flexible even when questions are challenging, and has alternative strategies
MATHEATICAL PRACTICES
1 Make sense of problems and persevere in solving them
3 Construct viable arguments and critique the reasoning of others
4 Model with mathematics
5 Use appropriate tools strategically
6 Attend to precision

ACTIVITY SUMMARY
Students build their conceptual understanding of mathematical vocabulary by defining terms, making a pictorial representation, and making a real-life connection. This graphic organizer is called a Verbal Visual Word Association (VVWA).

TIME: 10 minutes when introducing the activity, 5 minutes when revisited

ACTIVITY IN ACTION
1. Explain the activity to the students.
2. Students are given a term or phase. Without looking up the term or phrase they complete the VVWA.
3. Students share their VVWA with at least two other students.
4. Students revisit their VVWA and update it based upon their conversations.

ASSESSMENT
- Can the students make realistic real-life connections?
- Are the students able to update their VVWAs based upon their conversations with other students?

EXTENSIONS
- VVWA Quick Draw: Play a game where student teams race to complete a VVWA, but they start with the real-life connection (#4) and work their way backwards. The audience has to guess the term or phrase as they complete the VVWA. Points are awarded based upon the box the team is completing when the audience guesses the term or phrase. Box #1 is 10 points; box #2 is 20 points and so on.
- Make a VVWA Booklet: This can be a great study tool, resource and a way for teachers and students to track progress over time.

FAQ
Q: How can I differentiate this activity?
A: You can differentiate this activity by providing students or groups with different terms based upon identified and targeted math terminology. You can also have students working in small-groups to work on different sections of the VVWA based upon their areas of interest. For example, an artistic student could be the one to sketch out a real-life connection, but a student who likes to write might work on the definition.

NAME: _____   DATE: _____

Sample VERBAL VISUAL WORD ASSOCIATION (VVWA)

1) Term or Phrase	3) Pictorial Representation
percent	50% of the circles are shaded ○ ○ ○ ● ● ●
2) Definition	4) Real-life Connection
A percent is a special kind of ratio that has a part/whole relationship (like a fraction). But with a percent the whole is always 100.	I love it when I can find shoes that are 20% or more off. I can really save some money then. So if the shoes would normally cost $40, with a 20% discount I would pay $8 less.
Teacher Notes/Peer Comments	

#15 REPRESENTING THE OPERATION

LEARNING OBJECTIVE
Students will be able to identify operations to use to solve word problems by visualizing the situation.

GUIDING QUESTIONS
• How does your mathematical sketch justify or prove a particular operation? • Could the inverse operation be used? If so, would that change your mathematical sketch? Why? How?

MATERIALS
• word problem • Representing Operations Template

TEST-SAVVY SKILLS
• Manipulates mathematical ideas as applied to real-world contexts • Generates their own problems & solutions • Discusses/critiques solutions • Seeks out, identifies, explains, and replicates errors as tools for learning • Perseveres, is flexible even when questions are challenging, and has alternative strategies

MATHEMATICAL PRACTICES	
1	Make sense of problems and persevere in solving them
2	Reason abstractly and quantitatively
3	Construct viable arguments and critique the reasoning of others
4	Model with mathematics
5	Use appropriate tools strategically
6	Attend to precision
7	Look for and make use of structure
8	Look for and express repeated regularity in reasoning

ACTIVITY SUMMARY
Students work to figure out what operation(s) can be employed to solve the problem by making mathematical sketches to visualize (model) the mathematics and the operation(s).

TIME: 20 minutes when introducing the activity, 10 minutes when revisited

SET UP
1. Select 4 to 6 problems for the class.
2. Arrange students into small-groups and determine the problems that each group will get.

ACTIVITY IN ACTION
1. Students read the problem given to their group.
2. Students discuss the operation(s) that they think are involved and explain their rationale the group.
3. Once the group agrees on one operation, they then sketch out or make a math model to represent how they see the operation reflected in the context of the problem.
4. After the first operation has been visualized the group tries to determine if another operation is involved. If the group agrees that another operation is involved they repeat step #3.
5. Once a group completes the sketches for their problem, they join with another group that had the same problem to compare ideas.
6. Bring the class back together to discuss the arguments that they used to convince others of a particular operation.

ASSESSMENT
- Can the students determine the operation(s) to use?
- Was the rationale used conceptual, showing a deep mathematical understanding or based upon a "key word" strategy or non-mathematical connection?

EXTENSIONS
- Make a Game: Play the "Operations Game" where students are given two of the following symbols on cards: +, -, x, ÷. They are presented with a problem and have to place one of their symbols on the problem. In order to keep the problem, they have to justify why they are placing that symbol on the problem. If they cannot justify the placement of their symbol, then another student can steal the problem by justifying any symbol that they want. The winner is the student who gets rid of all of their symbols.

FAQ
Q: My students are struggling to see the operations, much less sketch it out. What can I do?
A: One idea is to work backwards. Tell them to assume that all of the operations are involved and they have to prove how each operation is possible given the situation. Another idea is to revisit previously solved problems and have students visualize those operations.

Sample REPRESENTING THE OPERATION

MATH PROBLEM
Ms. Jackson was about to go on a road trip, but first she wanted to go to the store to get a few things. She wanted to get some cookies and she saw that 1 pack cost $0.99. She decided to get 3 packs of cookies. Ms. Jackson also wanted to get a six pack of soda. The soda was on sale for 2-six packs for $4.00. If Ms. Jackson only had $10.00, would she have enough money to get what she wanted? Would she get any change? If so, how much?

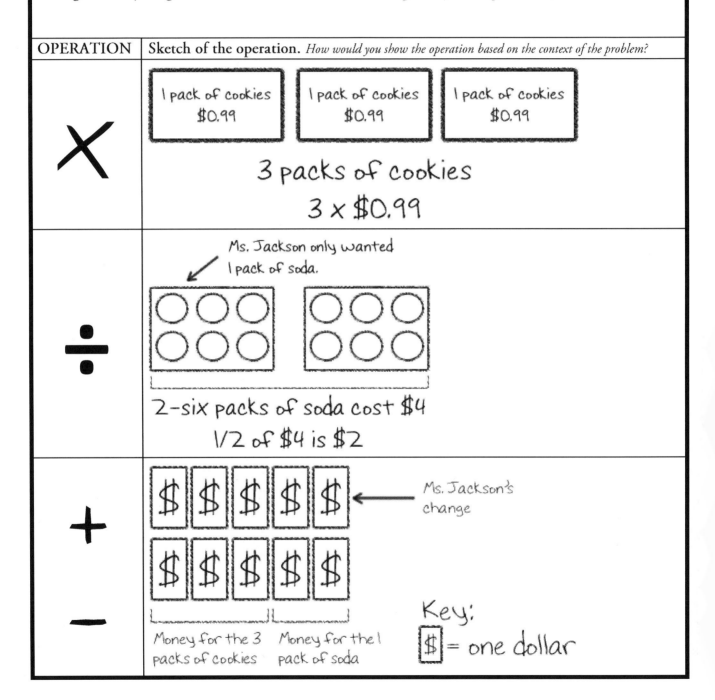

Section 4

THINKING LIKE A TEST-MAKER

Students are often unaware of the fact that exams are crafted to exploit common mathematical misconceptions. Exams operate on the premise that incorrect answers equate a lack of understanding of said concept(s) and/or skill(s) being tested. Students operate on the premise that the answer they get is the correct one.

The activities detailed in Section 4 provide opportunities for students to: 1) identify their own misconceptions, 2) use mistakes as a learning tool, and 3) collaborate with others to enhance their own learning. With consistent use, these strategies can help students become more actively aware of their own thinking and conscious of the kinds of common errors made by students just like them.

PONDER THIS...

- Trial and error learning is also valuable because it's intuitively simple. And mistakes, not correct answers, make us smarter (Jensen, 2005, p. 53).

- Metacognitive functioning is also facilitated by shifting from a focus on answers as just right or wrong to a more detailed focus on "debugging" a wrong answer, that is, finding where the error is, why it is an error, and correcting it (Donovan & Bransford, 2005, p. 239).

- Piaget theorized that the cognitive state of disequilibrium occurs when a person's existing understandings do not enable them to fully understand a problem or situation. Disequilibrium jumpstarts cognitive growth, as the brain works to re-establish equilibrium (understanding).

- Students solving a mathematics problem in small groups use cognitive behaviors and processes that are essentially similar to those of expert mathematical problem solvers (Artz and Armour-Thomas, 1992).

LEARNING OBJECTIVE	# #16 EVALUATING THE CHOICES

LEARNING OBJECTIVE

Students will be able to evaluate and discuss mathematically choices on selected response (multiple-choice) questions.

GUIDING QUESTIONS

- Why do you think the test-maker put this choice with this question?
- Based upon the choices, what are some typical misconceptions test-makers think students will have?

MATERIALS

- Template: Evaluate the Choices
- Exam question(s) with choices

TEST-SAVVY SKILLS

- Manipulates mathematical ideas as applied to real-world contexts
- Generates their own problems & solutions
- Discusses/critiques solutions
- Identifies common misconceptions related to concepts
- Develops visual memory of the exam format
- Is self-reflective, critical of work
- Seeks out, identifies, explains, and replicates errors as tools for learning
- Perseveres, is flexible even when questions are challenging, and has alternative strategies

MATHEATICAL PRACTICES

1. Make sense of problems and persevere in solving them
2. Reason abstractly and quantitatively
3. Construct viable arguments and critique the reasoning of others
6. Attend to precision

#16 EVALUATING THE CHOICES

ACTIVITY SUMMARY

Students look at the choices (distractors) and evaluate why the test-maker placed those items as choices.

TIME: 20 minutes when introducing the activity, 5 – 10 minutes when revisited

ACTIVITY IN ACTION

1. Explain to the students the purpose of the activity.
2. Students are presented with a multiple-choice problem and are asked to look at the choices.
3. Students should work independently for a few minutes to come to formulate their thoughts surrounding the question and the choices given.
4. Students are asked to work with a partner or in a small-group to evaluate and write about the choices given.
5. Bring the class together to discuss the choices and the student misconceptions that the test-makers are anticipating.

ASSESSMENT

- Can the students identify the misconceptions?
- Can the students provide a strategy or way to address noted mistakes or misconceptions?

EXTENSIONS

- Have students create or replicate mistakes based upon common student misconceptions. Time should be provided for students discuss and write about the mistakes that they created while thinking like a test maker.
- Have a "Distractor Creator" contest to see who would make the best test-item distractor. You could have multiple winners by including various domains and concepts or skills within each domain.

FAQ

Q: Should I focus my students on evaluating conceptual or computational errors?

A: Very good question. Your time should be balanced on both. Students need to address conceptual errors in order to clarify their thinking. Additionally, students need to see that the test-makers do think that they will make mistakes when computing numbers. Both of these areas can lead to rich discussions about alternative ways to check and/or show our thinking.

NAME: _____   DATE: _____

Sample EVALUATING THE CHOICES?

Directions: Read the problem and the choices (distractors). Explain why the test makers put each choice.

PROBLEM #1		
(Problem from NAEP Grade 4, 2011 Mathematics Assessment, 24% correct)		
The square has a perimeter of 12 units. 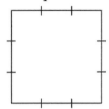 What is the area of the square?		
A) 6 square units	The test-makers put this choice, because… They added two sides (3 units + 3 units).	
B) 8 square units	A student would select this choice, because… They counted the 2 line segments on each side of the square.	
C) 9 square units	Students who pick this choices… The area is 9 square units (3 rows with 3 units in each).	
D) 12 square units	Students choosing this response, … They selected the same amount as the perimeter.	

PROBLEM #2	
(Problem from NAEP Grade 8, 2011 Mathematics Assessment, 33% correct)	
The point (4, k) is a solution to the equation $3x + 2y = 12$. What is the value of k?	
A) −3	
B) 0	
C) 2	
D) 3	
E) 4	

#17 MATCH THE CHOICES

LEARNING OBJECTIVE
Students will be able to make conjectures about the form and the mean of answers to exam questions.

GUIDING QUESTIONS
• Without solving the problem, explain how you know that this question matches to this set of choices?
• How would the choices change, if we changed the units in the problem?

MATERIALS
• Template: Match the Choices
• a multiple-choice problem

TEST-SAVVY SKILLS
• Manipulates mathematical ideas as applied to real-world contexts
• Generates their own problems & solutions
• Discusses/critiques solutions
• Identifies common misconceptions related to concepts
• Identifies/categorizes question types
• Develops visual memory of the exam format
• Develops the ability to skip around effectively, when needed
• Perseveres, is flexible even when questions are challenging, and has alternative strategies

MATHEATICAL PRACTICES
1 Make sense of problems and persevere in solving them
2 Reason abstractly and quantitatively
3 Construct viable arguments and critique the reasoning of others
4 Model with mathematics
6 Attend to precision

ACTIVITY SUMMARY
Students match the problems with the choices. This activity helps students anticipate the form and configuration of possible solutions prior to solving the problem.

TIME: 10 – 15 minutes when introducing the activity, 5 – 10 minutes when revisited

SET UP
1. Make small-groups and select about 10 multiple-choice problems for each group.
2. You could cut the multiple-choices away from the problems and place them in an envelope or Ziploc baggie or you could prepare a matching sheet (see then next page).

ACTIVITY IN ACTION
1. Explain the activity to the students.
2. Once students are given the materials, they work in small-groups to match up all the multiple-choice questions with the multiple-choice answers. It is expected that students are explaining their reasoning and arguing why they think a certain set of choices will match with a multiple-choice problem. Push students to decide on the choices without finding the solutions to the problems.

ASSESSMENT
- How do the students justify matches?
- Do the students start to speculate about the form of the answer upon reading the problem?

EXTENSIONS
- Math Centers: Combine this activity with other 15-minute Test-Savvy activities for small-group instruction.
- Have students create their own "Multiple-Choice Matching Game" for points.
- Present students with one problem and a set 3 multiple-choice problem sets. One of the sets should not belong. You want the students to determine which set does not belong and why.
- Have students identify the question category (see activity #5).

FAQ
Q: Do I always have to use multiple-choice questions?
A: No. You could use constructed response questions and have the students match them to solutions. This is great when you have a collection of student work samples.

NAME: _____   DATE: _____

Sample MATCH THE CHOICES

Directions: Match the questions with the multiple-choices.

Question	Choices
Which of the following equals 68 cents?	A. 47 C. 38 B. 21 D. 37
Which letter below does not contain a line of symmetry?	A. 150 and 125 C. 140 and 125 B. 144 and 119 D. 140 and 115
Look at the pattern below. What number is missing? 4, 8, 12, ___, 20	A. 3:15 B. 9:15 C. 3:45 D. 9:45
What time is shown on the clock?	A. 3 quarters and 3 pennies B. 2 quarters, 1 dime, 1 nickel, and 3 pennies C. 2 quarters, 2 dimes, and 3 pennies D. 3 quarters, 1 dime, and 3 pennies
Find the perimeter of the rectangle below. 9 cm 2 cm	A. M C. E B. F D. Y
What two numbers are missing from the pattern? 150, 145, _____, 135, 130, 125, 120, _____	A. ½ B. ¼ C. 1/3 D. 2/3
What fractional part of the circle below is shaded?	A. 20 B. 24 C. 16 D. 30
ANNA'S PEN COLLECTION <table><tr><th>Type of Pen</th><th>Number of Pens</th></tr><tr><td>Gel</td><td>26</td></tr><tr><td>Marker</td><td>12</td></tr><tr><td>Flex Grip</td><td>9</td></tr></table> How many pens does Anna have in her collection?	A. 22 cm C. 11 cm B. 18 cm D. 81 cm

Test-Savvy Math By Christine King, © 2013 CKingEducation, Inc.

#18 WHAT IS THE QUESTION?

LEARNING OBJECTIVE
Students will be able to generate mathematical questions based upon a given situation.
GUIDING QUESTIONS
• Why does your question(s) make sense for this situation? • How does creating questions help you better understand the situation?
MATERIALS
• Template: What is the Question • word problem without the question
TEST-SAVVY SKILLS
• Manipulates mathematical ideas as applied to real-world contexts • Generates their own problems & solutions • Discusses/critiques solutions • Identifies common misconceptions related to concepts • Develops visual memory of the exam format • Identify/Categorize question types • Perseveres, is flexible even when questions are challenging, and has alternative strategies
MATHEATICAL PRACTICES
1 Make sense of problems and persevere in solving them 2 Reason abstractly and quantitatively 3 Construct viable arguments and critique the reasoning of others 6 Attend to precision

ACTIVITY SUMMARY
Students create and answer questions based upon a given word problem scenario.

TIME: 10 – 15 minutes when introducing the activity, 5 – 10 minutes when revisited

ACTIVITY IN ACTION
1. Explain the activity to the students.
2. Present students with a word problem, but make sure that you have removed the question.
3. After reading the scenario, students work collaboratively to develop questions that could be answered given the scenario. You can prompt students by asking, "Hmmm? I wonder if we can create a question that would involve _____?"
4. Once several questions have been created have students select questions to answer and share their thinking.
5. Once students have answered a few questions discuss how answering one question might have led them to find the solution to other questions.

ASSESSMENT
• What kind of question do the students create?
• Can the students answer the questions created?

EXTENSIONS
• Have students create a question for given concepts. For example, you would have a scenario and you ask the students to make questions that involve the following concepts: multiplication, division, fractions.
• Make a Booklet of Student Created Questions: This can be a great study tool, resource and a way for teachers and students to track progress over time.
• Make mathematical sketches for each of the questions created.
• Math Centers: Combine this activity with other 15-minute Test-Savvy activities for small-group instruction.

FAQ
Q: My day is really packed and I don't even have 10-minutes for this? I see the benefit of this activity, but how might I incorporate it?

A: You are not alone in being squeezed for time. Instead of doing this in one day, what about keeping the problem scenario up the whole week posted on chart paper with Post-its handy. As students develop a question they jot it down on the Post-it. After a few days take all the questions and create a small-group center or incorporate into a whole class lesson.

Test-Savvy Math By Christine King, © 2013 CKingEducation, Inc.

NAME: DATE:

Sample WHAT IS THE QUESTION?

Directions: Read the problem and create questions that could be answered based upon the scenario given.

SCENARIO #1

Britney wanted to keep track of her family's weight for the next 6 months as they were doing a "Health Kick", her mother said. To get started she weighed all of her family members that she lived with. Her father weighed 230 lbs. Her mother weighed 145 lbs. Her 7 year old brother weighed 65 lbs. Britney weighed herself and found that she weighed 95 lbs.

1. How much more does Britney's father weigh than her mother?

Grades 3/4

2. What is the average weight of the family members?

Grades 4/5

3. How many times heavier is Britney than her brother?

Grades 6/7

SCENARIO #2

As a traveling nurse Ann has to travel to different locations each day for work. Her company will reimburse 60% of what she spends on gas. On Monday, Ann drove 10 mile to and from work. On Tuesday, she drove a total of 35 miles. On Wednesday, she went back to the same place she was on Monday. On Thursday, Ann had to drive 15 miles to work, but took a shorter route home, which was 12 miles. Ann worked from home on Friday.

1.

2.

3.

Test-Savvy Math By Christine King, © 2013 CKingEducation, Inc.

#19 WHAT ARE THE CHOICES?

LEARNING OBJECTIVE
Students will be able to generate choices for multiple-choice questions and explain how and why they developed those choices.
GUIDING QUESTIONS
• How does this choice make sense given the context?
• How do your incorrect choices reflect errors that students might make
MATERIALS
• Template: What are the Choices?
• a multiple-choice word problem
TEST-SAVVY SKILLS
• Manipulates mathematical ideas as applied to real-world contexts
• Generates their own problems & solutions
• Discusses/critiques solutions
• Identifies common misconceptions related to concepts
• Develops visual memory of the exam format
• Seeks out, identifies, explains, and replicates errors as tools for learning
• Perseveres, is flexible even when questions are challenging, and has alternative strategies
MATHEATICAL PRACTICES
1 Make sense of problems and persevere in solving them
2 Reason abstractly and quantitatively
3 Construct viable arguments and critique the reasoning of others
6 Attend to precision
7 Look for and make use of structure
8 Look for and express repeated regularity in reasoning

ACTIVITY SUMMARY
Students determine the choices (distractors) in a word problem, explain their thinking about the distractors, and the mistakes that other students would make.

TIME: 45 minutes when introducing the activity, 20 minutes when revisited

ACTIVITY IN ACTION
1. Present students with a word problem to work out or revisit a problem that the students have already resolved.
2. Discuss with the students the choices that the test makers used. Ask, "Why did the test-makers think a student would select this choice?"
3. Explain to the students that they are going to think like test makers and determine the choices.
4. Pair/Group students and provide each group with the problem(s) that they are going to work on.
5. Have students justify their choices to another pair/group.
6. As a whole group, discuss the typical mistakes that students might make and how to avoid them.

ASSESSMENT
- Can the student(s) create appropriate choices?
- Can the student identify and explain why a choice is incorrect?

EXTENSIONS
- Have students create choices for exam questions.
- Math Centers: Have each group work on a particular problem type and create specific distractors. For example, in a Change Unknown/Add To problem solving situation typical errors are: 1) adding all the numbers; 2) adding incorrectly; and 3) rounding the numbers
- Make a matching sheet with the choices and have students determine which choices match with the questions and the choices (see Activity 17: Match the Choices, pg. 67).

FAQ
Q: Is it ok to tell my students the kinds of choices that I want them to replicate?
A: Yes. This is a good way to introduce the activity, especially for younger grade levels who have limited exposure to standardized testing exam formats. You can brainstorm with your students the kinds of errors that students might make and have your students create distractors based upon the list generated.

NAME: _____   DATE: _____

Sample WHAT ARE THE CHOICES?

Directions: Read the problem and create choices (distractors). Explain your reasoning for each choice. Remember…
- 1 choice is correct
- 3 choices are incorrect and are mistakes that a student just like you might make

PROBLEM #1	
Edwin was asked to write and evaluate an equation for the following situation:	
The container had 3 raspberry muffins, six times as many blueberry muffins as raspberry muffins, and two apple muffins.	
Edwin wrote the following expression: 3 + 6 x 3 + 2 =	
Given the situation, what is the answer to the equation that Edwin wrote?	
A) 22	I put this choice, because… Students might add incorrectly.
B) 23	This is the correct choice, because… The situation is expressed by Edwin's expression, but he should have put parenthesis around the 6 x 3, because we have to find how many of each kind of muffin we have before we can add up all the muffins.
C) 29	A student would select this choice, because… They evaluated the expression going from left to right. So they added 3 + 6, and had a sum of 9. Then they multiplied 9 x 3 to get a product of 27. Finally, they added 27 + 2 to get a sum of 29. They did not pay attention to the situation. We cannot add 3 raspberry muffins to 6. We did not have 6 of any amount of muffins.
D) 45	Students choosing this response, … Would have added 3 + 6 and 3 + 2 separately, and then multiplied those sums.

PROBLEM #2	
Have a Go!	The temperature went from 3° degrees Fahrenheit to – 8° degrees Fahrenheit in a matter of 4 hours. By how much did the temperature change?
A)	
B)	
C)	
D)	

#20 MULTIPLE-CHOICE IN MINUTES

LEARNING OBJECTIVE
Students will be able to identify and reflect on how they respond to timed exam situations.
GUIDING QUESTIONS
• What kinds of questions were you able to do quickly and correctly?
• What are some of the strategies that you used to figure out answers?
• Which type of questions takes you longer to complete? Why?
MATERIALS
• Template: Bubble Sheet, Multiple-Choice in Minutes Reflection
• 3 – 4 multiple-choice problems
TEST-SAVVY SKILLS
• Manipulates mathematical ideas as applied to real-world contexts
• Generates their own problems & solutions
• Discusses/critiques solutions
• Identifies common misconceptions related to concepts
• Develops visual memory of the exam format
• Develops the ability to skip around effectively, when needed
• Is self-reflective, critical of work
• Analyzes data and identifies personal trends
• Perseveres, is flexible even when questions are challenging, and has alternative strategies
MATHEATICAL PRACTICES
1 Make sense of problems and persevere in solving them
2 Reason abstractly and quantitatively
3 Construct viable arguments and critique the reasoning of others
6 Attend to precision

ACTIVITY SUMMARY

Students build stamina and endurance by working on a series of targeted multiple-choice problems. Students also reflect on the types of questions that are more challenging for them and develop strategies to address specific problem types or conceptual areas.

TIME: 30 – 45 minutes when introducing the activity, 15 – 20 minutes when revisited

SET-UP

1. Arrange students into groups of 3 to 4 students.
2. Determine problem sets for each group.
3. Place problems face down on each desk.

ACTIVITY IN ACTION

1. Explain the Multiple-Choice in Minute process to students.
2. Explain how to use the Bubble Sheet.
3. Say, "Ready, Set, Go!" to begin the first problem.
4. Say, "Freeze!" to have students stop after the allotted time.
5. Have students rotate (clockwise or counter-clockwise) to the next problem.
6. Repeat steps 3 to 5 until all the problems are complete for that group.
7. Students turn-over all the problems and have students discuss and justify their choices.
8. Students reflect on the problems that were easy or challenging for them using the "Multiple-Choice in Minutes Reflection Sheet".

ASSESSMENT

- Can the student identify problems that are challenging for them?
- Can the student determine a strategy for resolving challenging problems?

EXTENSIONS

- Collaborative Multiple-Choice in Minutes: Students work in homogeneous pairs to solve multiple-choice problems.
- Multiple-Choice in Minutes Instructional Videos: Using the strategies outlined on the "Multiple-Choice in Minutes Reflection Sheet," students create "How-to" videos to advise other students on how to do this kind of problem in the allotted time.

FAQ

Q: Using the terms, "Ready, Set, Go" will make my students nervous. How can I help alleviate their anxiety? Should I not say, "Ready, Set, Go"?

A: The reality is that most people get nervous during testing situations. It is part of our bodies' natural response to a challenge or unfamiliar situation. The purpose of saying, "Ready, Set, Go" is to help our students internalize and accept these feelings and the process, but know that they can handle it and will be ok.

Q: How many minutes should I give my students per question?

A: For a general education class the time per question should be based upon the time given for the exam divided by the number of questions on the exam. For example, if students have 60 minutes to complete 30 questions (60/30), they would have 2 minutes per question. Make adjustments for students who are afforded additional time.

Sample MULTIPLE-CHOICE IN MINUTES

Bubble in your answers below:

[Bubble sheet with answers: 3-C, 5-D, 12-A marked]

MULTIPLE-CHOICE IN MINUTES REFLECTION SHEET

Name: Malcolm   Date(s): Jan. 8th

Question #	Your Choice	Level of Difficulty	Completion Time	Strategy Used	Group Choice
3	C	● Easy ○ Medium ○ Hard	● About 30 seconds ○ Almost 1 minute ○ About a 1 ½ minutes ○ About 2 minutes ○ I did not complete the question	○ I guessed ○ I used draw a picture ○ I used a table/chart/diagram/number line ● I looked at the numbers in the problem did an operation ○ Other:	B
5	D	○ Easy ○ Medium ● Hard	○ About 30 seconds ○ Almost 1 minute ○ About a 1 ½ minutes ● About 2 minutes ○ I did not complete the question	○ I guessed ● I used draw a picture ● I used a table/chart/diagram/number line ● I looked at the numbers in the problem did an operation ○ Other:	D
12	A	○ Easy ● Medium ○ Hard	○ About 30 seconds ○ Almost 1 minute ● About a 1 ½ minutes ○ About 2 minutes ○ I did not complete the question	○ I guessed ● I used draw a picture ○ I used a table/chart/diagram/number line ○ I looked at the numbers in the problem did an operation ○ Other:	A

REFLECTION

Which type of problem(s) gave you the most difficulty?	Discuss with your classmates some of the things that you could do about the questions that were most difficult for you. List some of the strategies suggested that you are willing to try out.
Problem #5 was the hardest for me and I got it right, but it took me about 2 minutes. I thought problem #3 was easy, but I got it wrong.	For problem #3, Tony said that I should make a list or draw a picture.

Test-Savvy Math By Christine King, © 2013 CKingEducation, Inc.

Section 5

VOCABULARY GAMES

Mathematics is a foreign language to all of us. Play is one of the ways that we can get better at speaking "math" and internalizing the concepts conveyed by mathematical terms.

The activities detailed in Section 5 provide opportunities for students to play with and talk about math terms using familiar childhood games. With consistent use, these strategies can help students build their mathematical vocabulary using fun and collaborative activities.

PONDER THIS...

- "I cannot teach anybody anything, I can only make them think." (Socrates)

- "What children can do together, they can do alone tomorrow" (Vygotsky, 1962).

- Research on students engaged in cooperative learning suggests that they achieve better when compared with students competing against each other individually (Walberg, 1999, Jensen, 2005, p. 100).

- Cooperative learning promotes creative thinking by increasing the number of ideas, quantity of ideas, feelings of stimulation and enjoyment and originality of expression in creative problem solving (Johnson & Johnson, p. 8).

- Students need to think about and discuss vocabulary terms and the concepts they represent in context to internalize them. Excerpt from *The Problem with Math is English*, Molina, 2012, p. 12.

LEARNING OBJECTIVE	# #21 SUNFLOWER WORD RIDDLE

LEARNING OBJECTIVE
Students will be able to reflect on the meaning of math vocabulary terms.
GUIDING QUESTIONS
• What do you know about this math terms?
• What other math terms come to mind when think about the term that we guessed?
• Where and when might we use this term in the real-world?
MATERIALS
• Template: Sunflower Word Riddle
TEST-SAVVY SKILLS
• Understands how math terms are related and relate terms to other math concepts
MATHEATICAL PRACTICES
1 Make sense of problems and persevere in solving them
3 Construct viable arguments and critique the reasoning of others
6 Attend to precision

#21 SUNFLOWER WORD RIDDLE

ACTIVITY IN ACTION
Students try to guess a word before the mathematical sunflower is erased. Similar to "Hangman".

TIME: 15 minutes when introducing the activity, 5 – 10 minutes when revisited

ACTIVITY IN ACTION
1. Explain to students how the game is played
2. Display the mathematical sunflower.
3. Decide on math term or phrase. Draw a dash for each letter of the term or phrase.
4. Tell the students the conceptual area or domain.
5. Begin taking guesses from the students.
6. Each correct letter guessed is written on the appropriate dash. Record incorrect letter or word guesses to serve as references for future guesses. Erase a part of the mathematical sunflower for each incorrect guess.
7. When the correct word or phrase is guessed, discuss what the word means.

ASSESSMENT
- Can the students discuss the word or phrases guessed in a mathematically appropriate manner?
- How long did it take for students to guess the word or phrase?

EXTENSIONS
- Make game into a math center.
- Have students develop clues or riddles for math terms.
- Make "word concept families" (e.g. multiplication, division, factor and product).

FAQ
Q: My students love this game, but how can I get them to focus on the mathematics, not just guessing the letters?

A: Limit the number of guesses and provide students with clues as to the word. For example, if the word were "factor", I might limit the number of guesses to 4 and give clues such as, "multiplication is involved," "they are only whole numbers," and "in division we have the divisor and the quotient instead." Each clue is more explicit and revealing than the one before.

Sample SUNFLOWER WORD RIDDLE

Category is: Circles

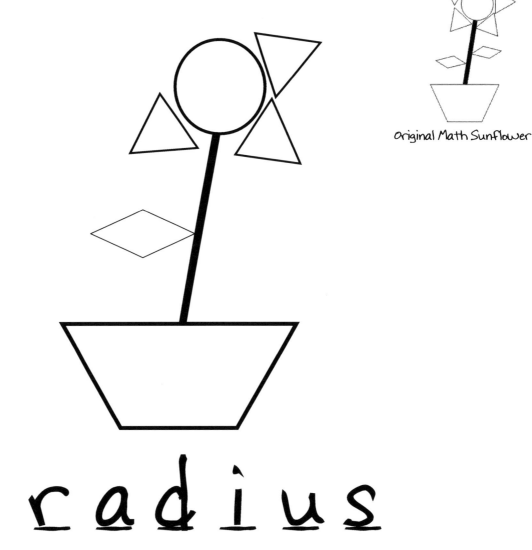

Original Math Sunflower

radius

Incorrect guesses:
(Three incorrect guesses were made, so 3 shapes were erased from the sunflower. The order in which the shapes are removed does not matter.)

p e c

#22 VOCABULARY TIC TAC TOE

LEARNING OBJECTIVE
Students will be able to discuss and make connections to math terms.

GUIDING QUESTIONS
• How do you know that your explanation is accurate?
• Can you tell some more details about your term?
• Can you restate what he/she said in your own words?

MATERIALS
• Template: Vocabulary Tic Tac Toe
• Math terms
• Reference materials (i.e. charts, glossary, notes, etc.)

TEST-SAVVY SKILLS
• Manipulates mathematical ideas as applied to real-world contexts
• Generates their own problems & solutions
• Discusses/critiques solutions
• Understands how math terms are related and relate terms to other math concepts
• Is self-reflective, critical of work
• Analyzes data and identifies personal trends
• Perseveres, is flexible even when questions are challenging, and has alternative strategies

MATHEATICAL PRACTICES	
1	Make sense of problems and persevere in solving them
2	Reason abstractly and quantitatively
3	Construct viable arguments and critique the reasoning of others
4	Model with mathematics
6	Attend to precision

ACTIVITY SUMMARY

Students play the game Tic Tac Toe where each cell in the grid contains a vocabulary term. In order to claim a cell, a player must identify the term in some way, such as defining it, using it in context or drawing a pictorial representation naming an associated term.

TIME: 45 minutes when introducing the activity, 20 minutes when revisited

SET UP

1. Create and copy the Tic Tac Toe Game Sheets by filling in the Tic Tac Toe Template.
2. Have blank Tic Tac Toe Templates available for students to create their own game.

ACTIVITY IN ACTION

1. Explain and model the game for the students.
2. Discuss reference resources that could be used.
3. Discuss ways that we can show and justify the meanings of terms.
4. Students play the game.
5. Student pairs create a Vocabulary Tic Tac Toe Game (and answer key) for others to play (*optional*).
6. Discuss with group terms that were particularly challenging and strategies to remember those terms.

ASSESSMENT

- Can the student associate the terms to nonlinguistic representations or in a real-world context?
- Is the student able to discuss the term beyond a standard definition found in a glossary?

EXTENSIONS

- Math Centers: Use student created games for Math Centers or during small-group instruction.
- Frayer Model/VVMA: Select words that are particularly challenging and create graphic organizer.
- Class Challenge: Make Tic Tac Toe teams that compete for the title of "Vocabulary Victors".
- Personal Glossary: Students record their solutions in their own personal book of terms.

FAQ

Q: How can I ensure that students are giving the correct definitions?
A: You could tell your students that Player "O" has to check Player "X's" definition by looking it up in a glossary or on a Math Word Wall. You could make groups of 3, with the third person being the "Checker." You could also provide students with an answer key.

Sample VOCABULARY TIC TAC TOE

PLAYED BY: Charlie and Lisa

CREATED BY: Tony

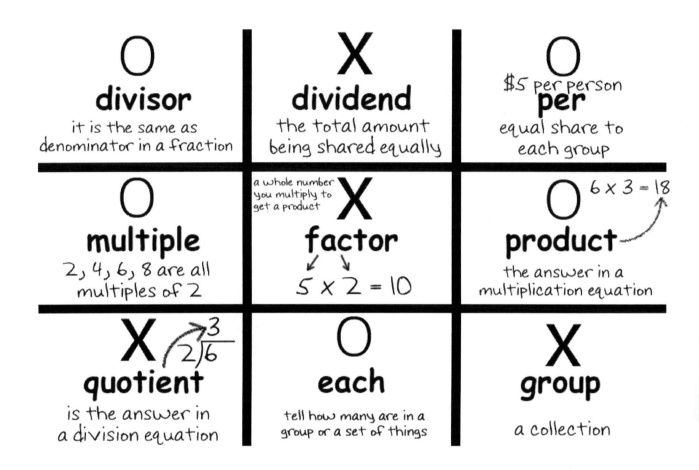

Extension Ideas:
- Create an acrostic poem using one of the words in the Vocabulary Tic Tac Toe
- Create a Frayer Model of one of the words in the Vocabulary Tic Tac Toe

#23 WORD CLUSTERS

LEARNING OBJECTIVE
Students will be able to associate sets of math terms with a real-life situation and mathematical symbol.

GUIDING QUESTIONS
- What mathematics can we use to make sense of this scenario?
- Why did you guess that term?
- How are these terms connected to this situation?

MATERIALS
- Template: Word Cluster
- a bank of word problem to get scenarios
- timer

TEST-SAVVY SKILLS
- Manipulates mathematical ideas as applied to real-world contexts
- Generates their own problems & solutions
- Discusses/critiques solutions
- Understands how math terms are related and relate terms to other math concepts
- Perseveres, is flexible even when questions are challenging, and has alternative strategies

MATHEATICAL PRACTICES
1. Make sense of problems and persevere in solving them
2. Reason abstractly and quantitatively
3. Construct viable arguments and critique the reasoning of others
4. Model with mathematics
6. Attend to precision

ACTIVITY SUMMARY
Students are put into teams and play for points by guessing words associated with a specific mathematical scenario. To get points, students give clues to their team members by drawing or acting out terms.

TIME: 15 minutes when introducing the activity, 10 minutes when revisited

SET UP
1. Use the story part or images from word problems to set-up the scenarios and generate word clusters for each scenario.
2. Use the "Word Cluster" template for small-group play or place scenarios on the board. Remember to hide the associated terms.
3. Decide on student teams.

ACTIVITY IN ACTION
1. A team selects a team member to read the scenario and act out or draw the associated words.
2. The selected team member reads the scenario to the group. The other team listens, but just watches.
3. Once the scenario is read, the selected team member has one-minute to act out or draw pictorial representations of the listed associated words.
4. As listed associated words are guessed, they can be written down and verbalized.
5. The game continues with the second team repeating steps 1 through 4.
6. The first team to reach twelve points wins.

ASSESSMENT
- Can the teams give appropriate clues?
- What terms do the students come up with? What does it tell us about what they know and understand?

EXTENSIONS
- Discuss the scenarios by focusing on why specific terms are in the listed associated words or what words could have been used instead.
- Have students make their own Word Cluster Cards and play with the class.
- Reverse the game and provide a list of associated words and have the students develop the scenario.

FAQ
Q: How would I use images as the scenario?
A: Images can convey mathematical information. For example, a circle can generate an associated word list such as: circumference, diameter, radius, chord and arc. The ability to look at an image and see/describe the underlying mathematical concepts begins with being able to say the mathematical terms associated with that image.

Q: Could I use something else other than words to describe a scenario or image?
A: Yes. You could use mathematical symbols, formulas, picture of real-life situations, physical objects (i.e. a 24-oz. water bottle), tables/charts, graphs, etc. The main thing is that students have to read or see something that will give them mathematical information.

Sample WORD CLUSTER CARD

Background Information	Associated Terms
Benny went to Home Depot to buy carpet to cover the floor of his bedroom.	Area multiplication measurement square feet length width
[square shape]	parallelogram rhombus quadrilateral rectangle parallel lines right angle
[gallon jug]	1 gallon 4 quarts 8 pints 16 cups Capacity Customary System

#24 SCHOOLYARD HANDCLAP GAME

LEARNING OBJECTIVE
Students will be able to generate and list math terms related to a particular conceptual area.
GUIDING QUESTIONS
• Do all of these words belong in this category? Why or why not?
• Can you explain how some of these math terms are connected?
MATERIALS
• a math word bank or Math Word Wall
• lyrics of the handclap game (see the next page)
TEST-SAVVY SKILLS
• Manipulates mathematical ideas as applied to real-world contexts
• Generates their own problems & solutions
• Discusses/critiques solutions
• Understands how math terms are related and relate terms to other math concepts
• Perseveres, is flexible even when questions are challenging, and has alternative strategies
MATHEATICAL PRACTICES
1 Make sense of problems and persevere in solving them
3 Construct viable arguments and critique the reasoning of others
6 Attend to precision

ACTIVITY SUMMARY
Students use schoolyard handclap games to build and focus on math vocabulary and terminology.

TIME: 15 minutes when introducing the activity, 5 – 10 minutes when revisited

ACTIVITY IN ACTION
1. Teacher explains to students that they are going to play a game that they might play in the schoolyard.
2. Show students the lyrics and model the rhythm/cadence.
3. Tell students the mathematical focus, i.e. "fractions".
4. Explain to the students the rules of the game.
5. Begin playing and record the terms that students say.
6. Discuss how these terms are related to the topic given.

ASSESSMENT
- Are the students calling out terms associated to the topic give?
- Can the students explain why the terms they called out fit the category given?

EXTENSIONS
- Adapt other handclap games or have students invent a handclap game focused on math.
- Make a video of students playing handclap games. Replay for class and discuss why certain terms were more appropriate than others.
- Have students complete a "Word Square" (see Activity 9: Concept Square, pg. 47) by selecting four terms from the list that were generated during the game.

FAQ
Q: What if my students cannot generate any terms?
A: Schedule a time for this activity, let your students know a few days in advance when the game will be played and provide them with reference resources to review in preparation for the game.

Q: Where can I get more handclap games?
A: Seek out the assistance of your students and lower elementary school teachers, in addition to the availability of several books and websites that focus on handclap games. Your instructional focus should remain on helping students generate related math terms, while involving kinesthetic movement.

Sample CONCENTRATION 64

The chorus goes...

Concentration 👏 👏

64 👏 👏

No repeats 👏 👏

Or hesitation 👏 👏

I'll go first 👏 👏

I'll go second 👏 👏

Category is _____

Example of 4 students playing when the category is: **Quadrilaterals**

Concentration 👏 👏
64 👏 👏
No repeats 👏 👏
Or hesitation 👏 👏
I'll go first 👏 👏
I'll go second 👏 👏
I'll go third 👏 👏
I'll go fourth 👏 👏
Category is Quadrilaterals 👏 👏
Squares 👏 👏
Trapezoids 👏 👏
Has 4 angles 👏 👏
Has 4 sides 👏 👏
Equals 360 degrees 👏 👏
Same degrees as a circle 👏 👏
Rectangles 👏 👏
Has 4 vertices 👏 👏
Make two triangles when cut on the diagonal 👏 👏

Example of 3 students playing when the category is: **24**

Concentration 👏 👏
64 👏 👏
No repeats 👏 👏
Or hesitation 👏 👏
I'll go first 👏 👏
I'll go second 👏 👏
I'll go third 👏 👏
Category is 24 👏 👏
Is a whole number 👏 👏
Is a multiple of 2 👏 👏
Is a multiple of 4 👏 👏
Is a multiple of 6 👏 👏
Is a multiple of 8 👏 👏
Has 2 as a factor 👏 👏
Has 6 as a factor 👏 👏
Has 8 as a factor 👏 👏
I made by 20 + 4 👏 👏

#25 MYSTERY WORD

LEARNING OBJECTIVE
Students will be able to connect and associate clues given about a math term to determine the topic being discussed.
GUIDING QUESTIONS
• Based upon the clues given, what domain of math do you think we are talking about? • Why does that real-life connection make sense for this term?
MATERIALS
• Vocabulary terms on post-it, index cards, or written on the board • Reference materials (i.e. charts, glossary, manipulatives, etc.)
TEST-SAVVY SKILLS
• Manipulates mathematical ideas as applied to real-world contexts • Generates their own problems & solutions • Discusses/critiques solutions • Understands how math terms are related and relate terms to other math concepts • Perseveres, is flexible even when questions are challenging, and has alternative strategies
MATHEATICAL PRACTICES
1 Make sense of problems and persevere in solving them 2 Reason abstractly and quantitatively 3 Construct viable arguments and critique the reasoning of others 4 Model with mathematics 5 Use appropriate tools 6 Attend to precision

ACTIVITY SUMMARY
Students try to figure out a mathematical term based upon the clues that they are given by their fellow classmates.

TIME: 15 minutes when introducing the activity, 5 – 10 minutes when revisited

ACTIVITY IN ACTION
1. Select a student to guess the mystery word.
2. Select a word and show it to the class, but do not show it to the selected student.
3. Without using the actual vocabulary term, the students give the selected student clues to help them figure out the word.
4. Record the clues given by the students.

ASSESSMENT
- Are the clues given appropriate for the term being discussed?
- Do the students remember the term a week after the activity was completed?
- What kind of nonlinguistic or real-world references were used?

EXTENSIONS
- Math Centers: Have students work in small groups of 4 to 6, rotating who is guessing the terms.
- Frayer Model/VVWA: Use the clues given to begin a Vocabulary Frayer Model (see Activity 14, pg. 59).
- Make a Riddle Booklet or PowerPoint: Record the clues given and make a booklet or PowerPoint that could be given to students to use at home or in math centers.

FAQ
Q: How do I select which words to use?
A: Many states provide grade-level math vocabulary lists for teachers and families to access. This could be a good starting place to select words/terms. Also a review of released or sample state exams is a good way to identify "high frequency vocabulary terms" or "specialized terms" that are used. Teachers could use data to determine which words they need to focus on. Teachers could ask students which words they struggle with and incorporate these words. Teachers could also use words from their current units of study or previous units of study. Another idea would be to sort words/terms in the categories of easy, medium or hard and focus on the medium to hard words/terms.

Q: How would I set this up to play in small groups?
A: You might have a stack of math vocabulary cards that the guesser can pick from. The card should be face down and when picked up by the guesser they should show the front of the card to the other player, but they should not look at the front of the card. You will also need a recorder to note the clues given. You could use a timer to keep the student on task and the game moving. If time runs out the guesser looks at the card.

Sample MYSTERY WORD

Activity Templates

Word Problem Rework	89
Rate My Work	91
Find and Fix My Error	92
Word Problem Carousel	94
Question Category	95
I Review	96
Two Arguments	97
Collaborative Explanation	98
Concept Square	99
Frayer Model Problem Solving	100
Rally Round the Problem	102
Match the Mathematical Picture	103
Show Me in Many Ways	104
Verbal & Visual Word Association	107
Representing the Operation	108
Evaluating the Choices	109
Match the Choices	110
What is the Question?	111
What are the Choices?	113
Multiple-Choice in Minutes	114
Sunflower Word Riddle	116
Vocabulary Tic Tac Toe	117
Word Clusters	119
Mystery Word	120

NAME: DATE:

WORD PROBLEM REWORK

ORIGINAL PROBLEM:

REWORK #1:

A)

B)

C)

D)

REWORK #2:

A)

B)

C)

D)

Test-Savvy Math By Christine King, © 2013 CKingEducation, Inc.

NAME: DATE:

WORD PROBLEM REWORK

ORIGINAL PROBLEM:

REWORK:

A)

B)

C)

D)

Explain:

NAME: _____   DATE: _____

RATE MY WORK

1. Solve the problem independently. You have _____ minutes.
2. Exchange your paper with a peer. Peers Name: _____
3. Use a rubric to evaluate and score your peers paper.
4. Explain to your peer the score you gave him/her.
5. On the back of this sheet, explain if you thought your score was fair. How could you improve your mark?

Problem	
Score:	Peer Explanation of Score Given:

NAME:	DATE:

FIND AND FIX MY ERROR

Directions:
1. The problem is incorrect. Read the problem.
2. Find the error.
3. Fix the error.
4. Explain the error that was made.
5. Use a different strategy to show the student how to do the problem correctly.
6. Tell the student how to avoid making that error in the future.

Target Problem:

Test-Savvy Math By Christine King, © 2013 CKingEducation, Inc.

Explain the Error:
_____
_____
_____
_____
_____
_____
_____

Explain and Show an Additional Strategy:
_____
_____
_____
_____
_____
_____
_____

Teacher Comments:

NAME: _____   DATE: _____

WORD PROBLEM CAROUSEL

Multiple-choice Question

Statement #1	
Statement #2	
Question	
Choice A	
Choice B	
Choice C	
Choice D	

Constructed Response

Statement #1	
Statement #2	
Statement #3	
Question	

NAME: _____   DATE: _____

QUESTION CATEGORY

Question	Category	Reason
	☐ Concepts ☐ Procedure ☐ Visual/Spatial Reasoning ☐ Use of Tools ☐ Vocabulary ☐ Symbols	
	☐ Concepts ☐ Procedure ☐ Visual/Spatial Reasoning ☐ Use of Tools ☐ Vocabulary ☐ Symbols	
	☐ Concepts ☐ Procedure ☐ Visual/Spatial Reasoning ☐ Use of Tools ☐ Vocabulary ☐ Symbols	

NAME: _____   DATE: _____

Test-Savvy Math By Christine King, © 2013 CKingEducation, Inc.

GROUP MEMBERS: _____   DATE: _____

iREVIEW ITEM ANALYSIS

Exam:	Date Given:	Grade Level:
Item #:	% Correct:	% Incorrect:

Misconception in Distractor Selected:
(What was the test-maker trap that most of the students fell into?)

Suggested Strategy to Avoid Trap:

Exam:	Date Given:	Grade Level:
Item #:	% Correct:	% Incorrect:

Misconception in Distractor Selected:
(What was the test-maker trap that most of the students fell into?)

Suggested Strategy to Avoid Trap:

NAME: _____ DATE: _____

TWO ARGUMENTS

Scenario

Argument #1	Argument #2

Decide and Defend

Whom do you agree with?	Why? *(Use Numbers, Words and a Model to defend your thinking.)* I agreed with…because…

Test-Savvy Math By Christine King, © 2013 CKingEducation, Inc.

STUDENT 1: _____ STUDENT 2: _____

STUDENT 3: _____ STUDENT 4: _____

COLLABORATIVE EXPLANATION

Original Problem

Written Explanation

_____
_____
_____
_____
_____
_____
_____
_____
_____
_____

Test-Savvy Math By Christine King, © 2013 CKingEducation, Inc.

NAME: _____   DATE: _____

CONCEPT SQUARE

Topic:

Topic:

NAME: _____ DATE: _____

FRAYER MODEL VOCABULARY

Definition	Facts

Term or Phrase

Examples	Non-Examples

Teacher Notes/Peer Comments

NAME: _____	DATE: _____

FRAYER MODEL PROBLEM SOLVING

Problem	Important Math Facts

Solution

Why Important?	Why Not Important?

Teacher Notes/Peer Comments

NAME: _____   DATE: _____

RALLY ROUND THE PROBLEM

1. **READ** the problem and identify any math terms used in the problem.
2. **RALLY** Round the Problem by writing other terms that can be associated with that problem.
3. **REFLECT** on the terms generated and highlight or circle the one that you think will help you solve the problem.
4. **RESOLVE** the problem.
5. **REVISIT** the solution by teaming up with other students who have similar problems and discuss your solutions.

THE PROBLEM	
MATH TERMS	WORK OUT THE PROBLEM
TEACHER COMMENTS	

Test-Savvy Math By Christine King, © 2013 CKingEducation, Inc.

MATCH THE MATHEMATICAL PICTURE

MATH PROBLEM	MATHEMATICAL SKETCH

NAME: _____ DATE: _____

SHOW ME IN MANY WAYS

Problem:

_____'s Way

_____'s Way

_____'s Way

_____'s Way

NAME: DATE:

SHOW ME IN MANY WAYS

Problem:

_____'s Way

_____'s Way

NAME: DATE:

Test-Savvy Math By Christine King, © 2013 CKingEducation, Inc.

NAME: DATE:

SHOW ME IN MANY WAYS

Problem:

_____'s Way

_____'s Way

NAME: DATE:

VERBAL VISUAL WORD ASSOCIATION (VVWA)

1) Term or Phrase	3) Pictorial Representation
2) Definition	4) Real-life Connection

Teacher Notes/Peer Comments

NAME: _____   DATE: _____

REPRESENTING THE OPERATION

MATH PROBLEM	
OPERATION	Sketch of the operation. *How would you show the operation based on the context of the problem?*

Test-Savvy Math By Christine King, © 2013 CKingEducation, Inc.

NAME: _____ DATE: _____

EVALUATING THE CHOICES?

Directions: Read the problem and the choices (distractors). Explain why the test makers put each choice. Remember…

- 1 choice is correct
- 3 choices are incorrect and are mistakes that a student just like you might make

PROBLEM #1	
A)	The test makers put this choice, because…
B)	A student would select this choice, because…
C)	Students who pick this choices…
D)	Students choosing this response, …
PROBLEM #2	
A)	
B)	
C)	
D)	

Test-Savvy Math By Christine King, © 2013 CKingEducation, Inc.

NAME: _____ DATE: _____

MATCH THE CHOICES

Directions: Match the questions with the multiple-choices.

Question	Choices

NAME: _____ DATE: _____

WHAT IS THE QUESTION?

Directions: Read the problem and create questions that could be answered based upon the scenario given.

SCENARIO #1
1.
2.
3.

SCENARIO #2
1.
2.
3.

NAME: _____ DATE: _____

WHAT IS THE QUESTION?

Directions: Read the problem and create questions that could be answered based upon the scenario given.

1.
2.
3.

Test-Savvy Math By Christine King, © 2013 CKingEducation, Inc.

NAME: _____   DATE: _____

WHAT ARE THE CHOICES?

Directions: Read the problem and create choices (distractors). Explain your reasoning for each choice. Remember…
- 1 choice is correct
- 3 choices are incorrect and are mistakes that a student just like you might make

PROBLEM #1	
A)	I put this choice, because…
B)	A student would select this choice, because…
C)	This is the correct choice, because…
D)	Students choosing this response, …
PROBLEM #2	
A)	
B)	
C)	
D)	

Test-Savvy Math By Christine King, © 2013 CKingEducation, Inc.

NAME: _____ DATE: _____

Bubble in your answers below:

Use this area to do your work.

Fraction Correct: /   Percent Correct:

Test-Savvy Math By Christine King, © 2013 CKingEducation, Inc.   114

MULTIPLE-CHOICE IN MINUTES REFLECTION SHEET

NAME: DATE(S):

Question #	Your Choice	Level of Difficulty	Completion Time	Strategy Used	Group Choice
		o Easy o Moderate o Hard	o About 30 seconds o Almost 1 minute o About a 1 ½ minutes o About 2 minutes o I did not complete the question	o I guessed o I used drew a picture o I used a table/chart/diagram/number line o I looked at the numbers in the problem did an operation o Other:	
		o Easy o Moderate o Hard	o About 30 seconds o Almost 1 minute o About a 1 ½ minutes o About 2 minutes o I did not complete the question	o I guessed o I used drew a picture o I used a table/chart/diagram/number line o I looked at the numbers in the problem did an operation o Other:	
		o Easy o Moderate o Hard	o About 30 seconds o Almost 1 minute o About a 1 ½ minutes o About 2 minutes o I did not complete the question	o I guessed o I used drew a picture o I used a table/chart/diagram/number line o I looked at the numbers in the problem did an operation o Other:	
		o Easy o Moderate o Hard	o About 30 seconds o Almost 1 minute o About a 1 ½ minutes o About 2 minutes o I did not complete the question	o I guessed o I used drew a picture o I used a table/chart/diagram/number line o I looked at the numbers in the problem did an operation o Other:	

REFLECTION

Which type of problem(s) gave you the most difficulty?	Discuss with your classmates some of the things that you could do about the questions that were most difficult for you. List some of the strategies suggested that you are willing to try out.

SUNFLOWER WORD RIDDLE

  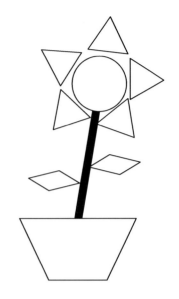

 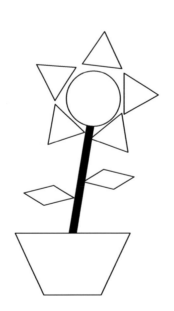 

VOCABULARY TIC TAC TOE

PLAYED BY: _____

CREATED BY: _____

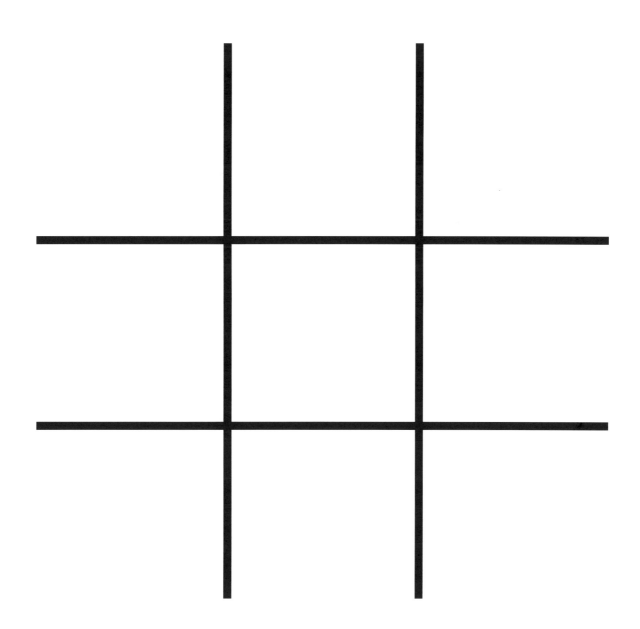

Extension Ideas:
- Create an acrostic poem using one of the words in the Vocabulary Tic Tac Toe
- Create a Frayer Model of one of the words in the Vocabulary Tic Tac Toe

MATH TIC TAC TOE

PLAYED BY: _____

CREATED BY: _____

Extension Ideas:
- _____
- _____

WORD CLUSTER CARD

Background Information	Associated Terms

MYSTERY WORD RECORD SHEET

Clues Given	Possible Words
Word: _____	
Word: _____	
Word: _____	
Word: _____	

Appendix

Test-Savvy Getting Started Action Planner — 123

Sample Test-Savvy Getting Started Action Planner — 125

Test-Savvy Teacher Data Tracking Sheet — 127

Test-Savvy Student Survey — 128

Test-Savvy Student Survey Instructions for Implementation — 129

Online Common Core State Standards Instructional and Assessment Resources — 130

Evidence-Centered Design Assessment Claims — 131
(Smarter Balanced and PARCC)

Interview with Christine King for "Guided Math" by Dr. Nicki Newton — 132
Dr. Nicki's Guided Math Blog (http://guidedmath.wordpress.com)

TEST-SAVVY GETTING STARTED ACTION PLANNER

Teacher:	Grade/Class:	Date:

1. **STUDENT DATA:**
   What are your areas of challenge for your students? How do you know?

2. **DECIDE ON LEARNING OBJECTIVE, TEST-SAVVY SKILLS AND/OR MATHEMATICAL PRACTICE(S)**
   Review student work samples or conduct student interviews to determine specifically what concept or skill students need to focus on and foster.

3. **SELECT A STRATEGY**
   Look at the "Quick Glance" section (pages 18 – 19) to determine which strategy would better support the information gathered in Parts 1 & 2. Explain why you would select that strategy.

4. **GETTING READY TO IMPLEMENT**
   I have…
   - ☐ Read and understand the strategy that I am going to implement.
   - ☐ I have gathered all the materials that I need to implement the strategy.
   - ☐ I have done the task(s) that I will have my students complete to note student misconceptions and challenges to determine additional guiding questions that could be asked to help students clarify their thinking.

   The misconceptions that I anticipate are…   My strategies to address those misconceptions are…

   _____   _____

   _____   _____

   _____   _____

   _____   _____

Test-Savvy Math By Christine King, © 2013 CKingEducation, Inc.

5. EFFECTIVELY GROUPING STUDENT

How will you group students? I will group my students in the following ways:

- ☐ Interest
- ☐ Readiness Level
- ☐ Concept of Focus
- ☐ Identified Area(s) of Challenge
- ☐ Identified Area(s) of Strength
- ☐ Product(s) Being Produced
- ☐ Learning Objective
- ☐ Learning Style

- ☐ Heterogeneously
- ☐ Homogeneously
- ☐ Using Pre-Assigned Math Groups
- ☐ Randomly
- ☐ Self-Selected by Students
- ☐ In Pairs (2)
- ☐ Small-groups (3 – 4)
- ☐ Whole-Group

I am grouping my students in this way because…

6. ASSESSING STUDENT PROGRESS

Part A: What evidence will you look for as an indication of student progress?

Part B: What percent of your students showed evidence of making progress as indicated in Part A?

7. REFLECTING ON THE ACTIVITY

What went well? What would you adapt?

8. COMMIT TO REVISITING THIS ACTIVITY

How many times do you anticipate revisiting this strategy?

When next will you revisit this activity?

Sample TEST-SAVVY GETTING STARTED ACTION PLANNER

Teacher: Ms. Smith	Grade/Class: 4-403	Date: Nov. 13th

1. STUDENT DATA:

What are your students' areas of challenge? How do you know?

We recently completed series of school-wide benchmark assessments and one area that my students had the greatest difficulty with was interpreting remainders in a division problem (CCSSM 4.OA.3). The assessment had 3 questions on this standard and the average correct for that standard was 36%. I also looked at the results of some classwork that was done a few days prior to the exam on this topic and the majority of my students were not able to interpret the remainder in the context of a word problem.

2. DECIDE ON LEARNING OBJECTIVE, TEST-SAVVY SKILLS AND/OR MATHEMATICAL PRACTICE(S)

Review student work samples or conduct student interviews to determine specifically what concept or skill students need to focus on and foster.

I conducted math interviews with a few of my students and noted that they were not relating the context to their calculations. They were able to get an answer, but they did not understand how to relate their answer to the context. The test-savvy skills that I think I need to focus on are: #1 Manipulates mathematical ideas as applied to real-world contexts, #3 Discusses/critiques solutions, and #10 Seeks out, identifies, explains, and replicates errors as tools for learning, because they need to actively think about answers in a given context.

3. SELECT A STRATEGY

Look at the "Quick Glance" section (pages 18 – 19) to determine which strategy would better support the information gathered in Parts 1 & 2. Explain why you would select that strategy.

I am going to use the "Find and Fix My Error" strategy because I have student work with errors and it will help them be more aware of some of the mistakes that they are making.

4. GETTING READY TO IMPLEMENT

I have…

- ☑ Read and understand the strategy that I am going to implement.
- ☑ I have gathered all the materials that I need to implement the strategy.
- ☑ I have done the task(s) that I will have my students complete to note student misconceptions and/or challenges to determine additional guiding questions that could be asked to help students clarify their thinking.

The misconceptions and/or challenges that I anticipate are…

- I think students will have difficulty reasoning through/explaining the error.
- I think students will have difficulty coming up with an alternative strategy that could be used to show the problem.

My strategies to address those misconceptions and/or challenges are…

- Have students work with a partner to make a mathematical sketch of the situation, making sure they label all of the parts.
- At the start of the lesson, review and show different ways to model our thinking in mathematics.

5. EFFECTIVELY GROUPING STUDENT

How will you group students? I will group my students in the following ways:

- ☐ Interest
- ☐ Readiness Level
- ☐ Concept of Focus
- ☑ Identified Area(s) of Challenge
- ☐ Identified Area(s) of Strength
- ☐ Product(s) Being Produced
- ☐ Learning Objective
- ☑ Learning Style
- ☑ Heterogeneously
- ☐ Homogeneously
- ☑ Using Pre-Assigned Math Groups
- ☐ Randomly
- ☐ Self-Selected by Students
- ☑ In Pairs (2)
- ☐ Small-groups (3 – 4)
- ☐ Whole-Group

I am grouping my students in this way because…
We are focused on a single concept for this lesson and it is an identified area of challenge. I am going to use my pre-assigned math pairs, because the activity is new for the students and I don't want to add new groups at the same time. My pre-assigned math groups are heterogeneous and incorporate learning styles, but the students are not wide apart in terms of demonstrated ability. I am also grouping in pairs to allow each person to have a voice.

6. ASSESSING STUDENT PROGRESS

Part A: What evidence will you look for as an indication of student progress?
(Complete prior to implementation of the lesson.)

I am looking to hear students say things like:
"In this problem the remainder means…"
"They got the problem wrong, because…"
"Look at my sketch…it will show you…"

Part B: What percent of your students showed evidence of making progress as indicated in Part A?
(Complete after the implementation of the lesson.)

About 80% of my students were able to find and fix the error and use some of the language indicated in Part A.

7. REFLECTING ON THE ACTIVITY

What went well? What would you adapt?

The activity worked out really well. My students were engaged and most were successful in finding and fixing the error. Posting prompts to get students talking and showing a variety of ways to show their thinking really helped the students…I saw many looking back at the chart. Next time I will have a variety of problems ready for students to do and also present several different situations for remainders with division.

8. COMMIT TO REVISITING THIS ACTIVITY

How many times do you anticipate revisiting this strategy? I am going to keep doing this activity at least 2 to 3 times a month for the rest of the year.

When next will you revisit this activity? Next week on the same topic, but this time I will make math centers for students to rotate through to solve different problems.

TEST-SAVVY TEACHER DATA TRACKING

Test-Savvy Activity	Math Content Targeted by Strategy	Pre/Post Activity Data	Teacher Reflection
Word Problem Rework (Jan. 8th)	Commutative Property of Addition, adding triple-digit numbers (3.NB.1)	Pre-Implementation Data 40% on benchmark exam Post-Implementation Data 82% on unit exam	When questioned students were able to explain the Commutative Property when working with larger numbers. Students used more strategies to double-check their work.
		Pre-Implementation Data Post-Implementation Data	
		Pre-Implementation Data Post-Implementation Data	
		Pre-Implementation Data Post-Implementation Data	
		Pre-Implementation Data Post-Implementation Data	

TEST-SAVVY STUDENT SURVEY
INSTRUCTIONS FOR IMPLEMENTATION

The *Test-Savvy Student Survey* places students on a continuum for becoming test-savvy. Knowing where a student falls on that continuum can help teachers make more informed instructional decisions about how to differentiate instruction to best meet the needs of all students. Additionally, teachers can use the survey to measure student growth on the continuum.

The questions asked on the survey reflect both ends of the continuum. For example, students scoring high on questions 1, 2, 3, 7, and 9 are said to be "more test-savvy." These sets of questions are referred to as: Scale A. Whereas, those students scoring high on questions 4, 5, 6, 8, 10 are said to be "less test-savvy." These sets of questions are referred to as: Scale B. Please note: This survey is not suitable for students who have never taken a standardized test, under standardized testing conditions.

Use the following scoring guide to determine where your students fall on the continuum. Space is provided to indicate the names or percent of students at each level.

POINTS FOR SCALE A: Questions: 1, 2, 3, 7, 9

Intimidated by testing situations			Confident in a testing situation
5 – 9 Points	10 – 14 Points	15 – 19 Points	20 – 25 Points
Level 1	Level 2	Level 3	Level 4

POINTS FOR SCALE B: Questions: 4, 5, 6, 8, 10

Confident in a testing situation			Intimidated by testing situations
5 – 9 Points	10 – 14 Points	15 – 19 Points	20 – 25 Points
Level 4	Level 3	Level 2	Level 1

TEST-SAVVY STUDENT SURVEY

This is an informal survey to find out **what students do and feel when they are taking the "Big Math Test."**

School:	Grade Level *(circle one)*: 3 4 5 6 7 8	Date:
State:	Gender: Male / Female	Age:

Directions: Please read each statement and circle where you fall on a scale of 1 (NEVER) to 5 (ALWAYS).

STATEMENT	*Never*	*Rarely*	*Sometimes*	*Often*	*Always*
1. If it is allowed, I look through the entire test booklet before I begin taking the test.	1	2	3	4	5
2. Even when an exam is timed, I read the questions twice.	1	2	3	4	5
3. I show and label my work, sometimes using drawings or charts.	1	2	3	4	5
4. Exams make me nervous.	1	2	3	4	5
5. I try to finish the exam as quickly as possible.	1	2	3	4	5
6. I do all the test questions in order.	1	2	3	4	5
7. When taking an exam I skip around and do the easier questions first.	1	2	3	4	5
8. I skip or guess the answers to questions that I don't know.	1	2	3	4	5
9. Exams make me excited to show how much I know.	1	2	3	4	5
10. I do better when the teacher reminds me to do my best.	1	2	3	4	5

FOR TEACHER USE ONLY:

	Points	Level
Scale A:		
Scale B		

Test-Savvy Math By Christine King, © 2013 CKingEducation, Inc.

ONLINE COMMON CORE STATE STANDARDS INSTRUCTIONAL AND ASSESSMENT RESOURCES

PARCC (Partnership of Assessment of Readiness for College and Career)
Web: http://www.parcconline.org
Smarter Balanced Assessment Consortium
Web: http://www.smarterbalanced.org
Illustrative Mathematics
Web: www.illustrativemathematics.org
The Progressions
Web: http://ime.math.arizona.edu/progressions
Common Core Blog
Web: http://commoncoretools.me
Achieve the Core
Web: http://www.achievethecore.org
National Assessment of Educational Progress (NAEP)
Web: http://nces.ed.gov/nationsreportcard/itmrlsx/landing.aspx
Charles A. Dana Center CCSS Toolkit
Web: http://www.ccsstoolbox.com/parcc/PARCCPrototype_main.html
Turn on Common Core Math
Web: http://turnonccmath.net
North Carolina Unpacked Math Standards
Web: http://www.ncpublicschools.org/acre/standards/common-core-tools/#unmath

EVIDENCE-CENTERED DESIGN ASSESSMENT CLAIMS FOR THE COMMON CORE STATE STANDARDS

Overall Claim for Grades 3–8
"Students can demonstrate progress toward college and career readiness in mathematics."

Smarter Balanced
Claim #1 – Concepts & Procedures
"Students can explain and apply mathematical concepts and interpret and carry out mathematical procedures with precision and fluency."
Claim #2 – Problem Solving
"Students can solve a range of complex well-posed problems in pure and applied mathematics, making productive use of knowledge and problem solving strategies."
Claim #3 – Communicating Reasoning
"Students can clearly and precisely construct viable arguments to support their own reasoning and to critique the reasoning of others."
Claim #4 – Modeling and Data Analysis
"Students can analyze complex, real-world scenarios and can construct and use mathematical models to interpret and solve problems."

PARCC
Claim #1: Problem Solving (Major Work)
"Students can solve problems involving the Major work of the grade with connections to the practice standards."
Claim #2: Problem Solving (Additional & Supporting Work)
"Students can solve problems involving the Additional and Supporting work of the grade with connections to the practice standards."
Claim #3: Communicating Reasoning
"Students can express mathematical reasoning by constructional mathematical arguments and critiques."
Claim #4: Modeling of Problems
"Students can solve real-world problems by engaging particularly in the modeling practice."
Claim #5: Fluency
"Students can demonstrate fluency in the areas set for in the content standards for Grades 3 – 6."

* The Model Content Framework explains the Major, Additional & Supporting work and can be found at: http://www.parcconline.org/parcc-model-content-frameworks

GUIDED MATH >>

Moving forward, one small-group at a time.

Christine King on Testing, Test-Savviness, and the Impact of the Common Core State Standards on Testing by Dr. Nicki Newton (guidedmath.wordpress.com)

We are here today with Christine King, author of *"The Digits Game"* and *"N^3 No Naked Numbers"*. Christine also has a blog, where she says that she, "...rambles on about testing." Her new book titled, *"Test-Savvy Math: Fostering Thinking and Reasoning into the Test-Prep Process"*, is coming out soon and I wanted to talk to her about her motivation behind the book and the impact that she hopes the book will have on the test-prep process.

1. Why did you write a book about test-prep?

I would like to think that I did not write a book about test-prep. I dislike the notion of test-prep. That may be a shock to most people, but I wrote a book about good, research-based teaching strategies and how those strategies can be applied and used effectively in the test-preparation process. I wrote the book because I was tired of having schools ask me year-after-year, two months before standardized exams were to begin, "Christine, how should we prepare for the tests?" I wrote the book in the hopes that my own children and other children would have options and not be subjected to mindless test-prep.

2. What is your biggest concern in terms of how the book and the strategies outlined will be received?

I have two concerns, fears you could say. The first is that teachers and administrators expect these strategies to be a "magic pill" and that scores will skyrocket if they implement these strategies. That would be nice, but not realistic. The strategies outlined in Test-Savvy Math need to be a part of an overall balanced mathematics program and when used consistently, with data to drive instruction, they can help students become more test-savvy.

The second concern that I have is that teachers will only look at the strategies as preparation for a few days of testing. I have heard teachers say, while using these strategies, "We are doing this, because you have a test in a few months." Inside my head I am screaming, "NO, NO, NO! This is only partly about a test in a few months...but this is about thinking and reasoning in LIFE!"

3. What does it mean to be test-savvy?

Hmmm. I am not going to read the introduction of the book, because you could do that on your own. To be test-savvy means that you have a "can-do" attitude. You know that something might be challenging, but you know that you will be able to handle the challenge and figure out a way. Test-savviness is a mind-set for living in the 21st century. Test-savviness is about the mental preparation necessary to equip our students to face situations and structures that are unfamiliar and sometimes uncomfortable.

4. In your opinion, how is the Math Common Core State Standards impacting testing?

Aside from educators being in a tizzy? I see positive changes in the sense that teachers are more open to expanding their content knowledge in order to meet the expectations of the CCSSM. In the long run this will benefit students…you teach what you know. I also see confusion and frustration, because things are not clear, fully mapped out, and everyone only has access to pieces of the puzzle. It is a bumpy road right now and everyone…teachers, administrators, and students are feeling it. The exams are going to become more rigorous, requiring more strategic thinking, and will be more cognitively demanding. As Wiggins says the CCSS requires us to, "…teach for transfer."

5. What do you mean by "transfer" and how does that relate to test-savviness?

Transfer in an educational setting refers to the learners' ability to apply previous learning to a new and seemingly different situation. For example, at the K – 3 levels students are learning about the concept of addition and the base-ten system…we add ones with ones and tens with tens. By the time students are in the fourth or fifth grades they are learning about adding fractions and decimals. Think about the deep levels of conceptual understanding that would have occurred for a student to say, "Oh, this is just like adding whole numbers. We add like units with like units. So tenths go with tenths and fourths are added to fourths." How does that compare to the mantra of, "Line up the decimals."

Test-savviness promotes the kind of thinking and questioning necessary to help foster the collaborative environment needed to help students willingly tap into their prior knowledge. For example, the game "Mystery", which is activity #25 in the book, asks students to listen to the clues that their peers are giving them to figure out a specific math term. The students who are giving the clues are required to make real-life and mathematical connections by tapping into their prior knowledge and transferring those understandings to this new situation.

6. What is your favorite strategy and why?

It changes. I loved the "Word Problem Rework" for a while. It is the strategy that started it all. I loved it when I saw students thinking about what numbers to use given the context. I loved when students were excited about solving the problems other students created. For a time the "Collaborative Explanation" excited me, because the students saw that they could write in math. I love all the vocabulary games, especially "Vocabulary Tic Tac Toe." The "School Yard Hand Clap Game" is the most challenging for me…I am not very musical, but I love that strategy, because I adapted it from the games I saw students playing. "Match the Math Picture" always amuses me when I see students critiquing the thinking of others. So which strategy is my favorite…it changes based upon how I see students thinking.

7. Where can we go to find out more about "Test-Savvy Math"?

Well the book will be out in Spring 2013, but I have a blog named, "Test-Savvy Math" at www.testsavvymath.blogspot.com. As you mentioned…those are my ramblings about testing and the test-savvy philosophy. I don't write posts on the blog as often as I would like…only when I am inspired or interviewing people from the field, but I have webinars posted and sample activities for people to view and download.

References

BOOKS

Allen, Janet. *Words, Words, Words: Teaching Vocabulary in Grades 4-12*. York, Me.: Stenhouse, 1999. Print.

Donovan, Suzanne, and John Bransford. *How Students Learn: Mathematics in the Classroom*. Washington, D.C.: National Academies, 2005. Print.

Jensen, Eric. *Teaching with the Brain in Mind*. Alexandria, VA: Association for Supervision and Curriculum Development, 1998. Print.

Marzano, Robert J., Debra Pickering, and Jane E. Pollock. *Classroom Instruction That Works: Research-based Strategies for Increasing Student Achievement*. Alexandria, VA: Association for Supervision and Curriculum Development, 2001. Print.

Surowiecki, James. *The Wisdom of Crowds*. New York: Anchor, 2005. Print.

Tileston, Donna Walker. *Teaching Strategies for Active Learning*. Thousand Oaks: Corwin, 2007. Print.

ONLINE RESOURCES

Kagan, S. *Kagan Structures: Research and Rationale in a Nutshell*. San Clemente, CA: Kagan Publishing. *Kagan Online Magazine,* Winter 2003. www.KaganOnline.com

Mislevy, Robert, Russell G. Almond, Janice F. Lukas. *A Brief Introduction to Evidence-Centered Design*. Education Testing Service (ETS), 2003. PDF.

PARCC. *PARCC Model Content Frameworks Mathematics Grades 3–1.*

Pearson Assessments. *PARCC Item Development – Memo to Janice Brown*. NCS Pearson, Inc. February, 17, 2012. PDF.

Smarter Balanced Assessment Consortium. *Mathematics Item Specifications Grades 3-5*. Measured Progress/ETS Collaborative April 16, 2012. PDF.

The Author

Christine Mulgrave-King is a K – 8 Math Consultant dedicated to helping teachers improve the craft of teaching mathematics. Christine has a Master's Degree in Instructional Technology and Media, Math, Science & Technology from the Department of Teacher's College, Columbia University. She began her career in education in 1993, as a Teach for America (TFA) core member, teaching sixth grade in NYC. In 2003, Christine branched out and began consulting for various schools in NYC, subsequently becoming a highly sought-after presenter and professional developer.

Other books and resources by Christine King are available at: www.ckingeducation.com.

Want training on how to use this resource in the classroom?

CKingEducation is available for on-site workshops, classroom demonstration lessons or online webinars on how to use *Test-Savvy Math: Fostering Thinking and Reasoning into the Test-Prep Process* in the classroom.

Want to show templates on an interactive white board?

An Adobe PDF Resource Pack of *Test-Savvy Math Templates* is available for purchase at www.ckingeducation.com and allows teachers to display templates for whole group interactivity.

Contact Us!

C. King Education, Inc.
Phone: 412-CKingEd
Web: www.ckingeducation.com
Email: info@ckingeducation.com

Made in the USA
Lexington, KY
07 July 2018